God's Word for Your Healing

Harrison House
Tulsa, Oklahoma

Unless otherwise indicated, all Scripture quotations are taken from the *King James Version* of the Bible.

"One Hundred Divine Healing Facts" is taken from *One Hundred Divine Healing Facts*, Copyright © 1983 by T.L. Osborn, Tulsa, Oklahoma.

Old Testament Hebrew research provided by David Michael. New Testament Greek research provided by Dick Mills.

3rd Printing
Over 23,000 in Print

God's Word for Your Healing
ISBN 0-89274-907-5
Copyright © 1993 by Harrison House
P. O. Box 35035
Tulsa, Oklahoma 74153

Contents

He sent His word, and healed them, and delivered them from their destructions.

Psalms 107:20

Introduction

It's been said that "healing is the children's bread." God promises us in His Word that Jesus died to bring to us not only salvation and eternal life — which is enough in itself — but also divine healing for our bodies. What does this mean? It means that *God wants you to be healed and He wants you to stay healthy*!

You may be asking, "But how do I know that it is God's will to heal me?" That is the exact reason why this book has been written. Even though there are more study Bibles and Bible commentary books being sold today than ever before, there is still too much confusion regarding God's promises to His children for healing. The confusion can end here.

The book you hold in your hands has been designed to show you the Scriptures that will help you stand in faith for your healing and prepare you to receive it. You will find every healing Scripture from the Bible. You will also find a 31-day healing devotional to help you walk out your faith in the area of healing, anointed teaching on God's provision for healing, and how to overcome hindrances to your healing. All this has been included to inspire and encourage you daily.

God wants you to be healed! His Word says it is for you! *God's Word for Your Healing* is your source for Godly wisdom and unlocking the healing power found in the Bible!

*W*e see, from almost every conceivable angle throughout the Scripture, that there is no doctrine more clearly taught than it is God's will to all who have need of healing, and that they may fulfill the number of their days, according to His promise.

F.F. Bosworth

1
Greek And Hebrew Word Studies on Healing

Old Testament — *Rapha*

Heal (*rapha*) me, O Lord, and I shall be *healed* (*rapha*); save me, and I shall be saved. . . .

Jeremiah 17:14

New Testament — Therapeuo

There came a multitude out of the cities round about unto Jerusalem, bringing sick folks, and them which were vexed with unclean spirits: and they were healed (*therapeuo*) every one.

Acts 5:16

Healing — *Rapha*

Heal (*rapha*) me, O Lord, and I shall be healed (*rapha*); save me, and I shall be saved.

Jeremiah 17:14

The name of God is such that His heart intensely yearns to heal and repair His creation. Mankind has become so terribly marred by sin, sorrow, evil and the countless disorders which plague the physical, emotional, mental, behavioral and spiritual components of man's being.

All creation in general — the human race in particular — is groaning and travailing under the complex burdens which result from sin and the Fall. Those burdens include sickness, birth defects, emotional illness, compelling behavioral dysfunctions, death, a host of inexpressible

11

heartaches known to man, alienation, loneliness, famine, bereavement, loss, futility and everything else which is contrary to God's design and desire for creation!

It is for God's own sake that He steadfastly desires to repair these blotches on His beautiful handiwork. Since these griefs abound worldwide, healing, repair and restoration can never be far from God's thoughts. Restoring creation to its proper function and beauty, and repairing man — the crowning glory of His works — is a desire which originates solely in God's heart.

Thus, He has pledged repeatedly, in both Testaments, that He will completely repair the earth and all creation. He will heal the world's uncountable sorrows and restore the human race to a position of nobility. He will banish sickness and destroy finally and forever His great enemy, Death. God is One Who repairs what He has made, not One Who is inclined to abandon the work of His own hands.

From this broad overview of the Lord's announced plan to remedy the ills of creation, we shall now focus upon His specific healing of human ills as seen in the biblical record.

The Hebrew word for "heal" is the verb *rapha* (pronounced "raw-faw'"), #7495 in *Strong's*, which means to repair, restore health, heal, mend, fix, cure.

Rapha occurs more than sixty times in the Old Testament. Its first occurrence is in Genesis 20:17. Abraham prayed to God on behalf of Abimelech, and God healed him and his household.

Rapha occurs in many famous verses, such as Psalm 103:3, referring to the Lord **"who forgiveth all thine iniquities; who** *healeth (rapha)* **all thy diseases."** And Psalm 107:20: **"He sent His word, and** *healed (rapha)* **them."** Its most majestic occurrence is in Isaiah 53:5, which tells us we are healed by the stripes of God's sacrificed Lamb, Jesus the Messiah.

In the Book of Leviticus (*rapha*) is used to describe healing from sickness or plague such as leprosy. (Lev. 13:18,37; 14:3,48.)

Some unscholarly disputers of the validity of divine healing have gone out on a limb to maintain that "healing" does not refer to physical healing in the Bible. Aside from the basic nonsense of such a stance, we note that leprosy is a *physical* condition whose cure can only be *physically* verifiable.

Additionally, the participle form of *rapha* is *rophe* ("ro'-fay") which means doctor, physician. Jeremiah 8:22 and 2 Chronicles 16:12 clearly portray the work of physicians or doctors as healers, or at least as specialists who are supposed to be able to bring healing. The Lord applies this word to Himself in Exodus 15:26 when He says, ". . .**I am the Lord that healeth thee.**" In other words, "I am Jehovah, your *rophe*," — that is, your Doctor, your Physician and your Healer.

The majority of occurrences of the *rapha* word group in the Scripture refer to physical healing. However, some of the other references where *rapha* is found will shed greater understanding on this powerful word.

For instance, in the well-known promise — Second Chronicles 7:14 — God declares that the repentance and prayer of His people will result in their land being healed! Relatively few saints seem to have a clear grasp of how intensely God yearns to heal the earth. But it is His splendid jewel which reflects His glory. Isaiah 6:3 says, ". . . **the whole earth is full of his glory.**" Thus, whenever the earth is scarred, destroyed or blighted, it is an assault on His handiwork.

In Second Kings 2:22 Elisha "healed" the undrinkable, poisoned water in the spring at Jericho, and these waters remained permanently healed. Compare the healing of the waters in the Dead Sea. (Ezek. 47:9.)

Psalm 147:3 portrays another use of the word *rapha* by declaring God heals the "broken in heart." Here is a real condition, one of the most serious a person can face. Yet it cannot be seen with the eye or measured on any medical instrument. It urgently requires healing, and only the Lord can satisfactorily heal this condition called "broken-heartedness."

A similar concept is found in Jeremiah 30:17 where the Lord promises healing for Israel's wounds. The most difficult wounds to heal are the kind no one can see.

A related concept is found in Jeremiah 3:22 where God pledges to "heal" His people of their backslidings. Here we see an excellent example of a behavioral disorder which God sees as being in need of healing, cure, repair and restored health. Three Scripture verses — Lamentations 2:13, Jeremiah 6:14 and 8:11 — refer to the "hurt" in God's people that has not been healed.

Rapha is considered to be the opposite of "tearing" (Hos. 6:1), "wounding" (Deut. 32:39) and "smiting" (Is. 19:22). There is a noun formed from *rapha* which is *marpe'* ("mar-pay'"), #4832 in Strong's, translated healing. Its most famous occurrence concerns the rising "**Sun of righteousness. . .with healing in his wings**" (Mal 4:2). It also occurs in such verses as Proverbs 4:22, 12:18 and Jeremiah 33:6.

One of the most beautiful uses of *rapha* is in Psalm 41:4. David says, "**Lord, be merciful unto me:** *heal (rapha)* **my soul; for I have sinned against thee.**" Let us note a few things which can be learned from this verse.

The human soul sometimes needs to be healed. Brokenness, disease or injury of the soul can be caused by sin, and an act of God's mercy brings healing to the soul.

An army of mental health personnel is overburdened as it tries to treat multitudes of mentally injured persons.

Sometimes these professionals, who are dedicated to helping the emotionally ill and traumatized, have successful results. And sometimes they cannot bring healing, as if the wounds are so great their repair is beyond the reach of human hands.

The Great Physician is equally comfortable healing both emotional and physical disorders. An old hymn states, "There is a balm in Gilead, to make the wounded whole. . .to heal the sin-sick soul."

The final example of *rapha* cited in this vein is in First Kings 18:30. Elijah "repaired" the altar of the Lord, which was broken down. English translators might use the words *fix, repair, restore, mend*. Yet the Hebrew word is *heal*. Elijah found God's altar in a state of disrepair and brokenness, and his heart yearned to restore it to its original wholeness and magnificence.

Similarly, the "healing" which God desires to bestow is for man's whole being. It involves repair of the physical body, soul, behavior, life, and even extends outward to nature itself.

As our vision for healing expands from healing of the sick to healing of ills wherever found, we will be more in line with the glorious plan of our Lord and God. Jesus *always* healed the sick — all of them — who came to Him. So we should *always* expect great miracles of physical healing. We should believe for greater, more astounding healings than have ever been recorded. And God desires entire nations to be healed. So should we!

Let us increase our vision. Let us intercede to see God's desires burst forth on this deeply troubled planet. The Lord made a provision in the heavenly city which shall descend, a provision to cure any illness that could possibly develop in Messiah's domain. He stated, ". . .**the leaves of the tree were for the healing of the nations**" (Rev. 22:2).

Greek Words Translated *Heal/Healing*
In the *King James Version*
Verbs

Diasozo ("dee-as-odze'-o), #1295 in *Strong's* — making thoroughly sound or whole.

> . . . and as many as touched (Him) were made perfectly whole *(diasozo)*.
>
> **Matthew 14:36**

Therapeuo ("ther-ap-yoo'-o"), #2323 in *Strong's* — to heal, cure, restore to health.

> Jesus went about all Galilee, teaching. . . preaching. . . and healing *(therapeuo)* all manner of sickness and all manner of disease among the people.
>
> **Matthew 4:23**

Iaomai ("ee-ah'-om-ahee"), #2390 in *Strong's* — to cure, to heal, to make whole.

> . . .by whose stripes ye were healed *(iaomai)*.
>
> **1 Peter 2:24**

Sozo ("sode-zo"), #4982 in *Strong's* — to make sound or to make whole.

> . . .he had faith to be healed *(sozo)*.
>
> **Acts 14:9**

Nouns

Therapeia ("ther-ap-i'-ah"), #2322 in *Strong's* — help a person receive healing; caring for a household.

> . . .he spake unto them of the kingdom of God, and healed them that had need of healing *(therapeia)*.
>
> **Luke 9:11**

Iama ("ee'-am-ah"), #2386 in *Strong's* — healing or effecting a cure.

> . . .to another the gifts of healing *(iama)* by the same Spirit.
>
> **1 Corinthians 12:9**

16

Iasis ("ee'-as-is"), #2392 in *Strong's* — the act of healing.

> . . . **and I do cure** *(iasis)* **today and tomorrow. . . .**
> **Luke 13:32**

Health

Soteria ("so-tay-ree'-ah"), #4991 in *Strong's* — health, soundness, safety.

> **for this is for your health** *(soteria)*. . . .
> **Acts 27:34**

Note: Later versions and newer translations use the word survival for health.

Hugiaino ("hoog-ee-ah'-eeno"), #5198 in *Strong's* — to be healthy or hygienically sound.

> . . .**that thou mayest prosper and be in health**
> *(bugiano),* **even as thy soul prospereth.**
> **3 John 2**

Health — *Therapeuo*

A major word used forty-four times for healing in the New Testament is *therapeuo* ("ther-ap-yoo'-o), #2323 in *Strong's*. Our English words *therapy* and *therapeutic* originate from this word. Using lexical tools and sources going back to antiquity, let us see how a serving word is associated with miracles.

The classical grammarians and language historians tell us *therapeuo* originally was a servant word. It is defined as: caring for, attending to, nurturing, waiting upon, serving in any beneficial capacity, helping, assisting, ministering to, providing for. It is related to *therapon* ("ther-ap'-ohn"), #2324 in *Strong's*, a menial domestic who attends to the needs of a household in a cherishing way.

In a large estate the household staff included all domestic servants and those whose function consisted of household maintenance. Also included were those who manicured the lawns and took care of the animals used for riding or plowing.

Therapeuo progressed to giving family members relief in time of sickness. It was associated with curing, healing, mending, restoring, treating medically and doing the work of a physician.

It is easy for a word with a 2,000-year history to change as the language, customs, idiom and usage change. Jesus' entry into the world changed *therapeuo* from natural methods of healing to miracles of healing.

Of the forty-four times *therapeuo* is used, two are in Revelation 13:2 and 12, describing the Tribulation beast that is healed (*therapeuo*). In Acts 17:25 the word is used to describe men worshipping idols. The *New International Version* reads, "...**he is not served by human hands.**"

In Luke 4:23 the word *therapeuo* is used of the medical profession: "...**Physician, heal thyself....**" In Luke 8:43, the woman with the issue of blood could not be healed by usual medical methods, but she was healed by Jesus.

Thus forty-one out of forty-four words refer to miraculous cures bestowed by Jesus and His disciples upon needy people.

Look at the progressive unfolding of the word *therapeuo* from:

(1)   serving your fellow man; to

(2)   tending sick humanity; to

(3)   medically treating the human race; to

(4)   miraculously healing sick people.

This sends us three messages:

1. The Servant of the Lord is fulfilling Old Testament prophecies by His healing miracles. In taking up the cause

of the helpless, Jesus authenticates Himself being God's suffering servant as prophesied by Isaiah.

2. Giving His followers authority to heal (*therapeuo*) all diseases demonstrates Jesus's power to break into our suffering world and give Christianity victory over the power of Satan (Luke 10:9,19).

3. Healings wrought in the name of the Lord in today's churches give evidence that the exalted Lord is actively present with His worshippers. He answers their prayers by demonstrating His power to heal all manner of sickness and all manner of disease.

Two ominous figures — sin and suffering — dogged the footsteps of Adam and Eve as they left the Garden. Jesus took both into focus when He died for our sins and our sicknesses. Psalm 103:3 says He forgives all our sins and heals all our diseases.

In the Passover the lamb served two purposes for God's people. Its blood covered sin's judgment, and eating the Passover lamb gave the Israelites power and vitality to march out of Egypt. Psalm 105:37 says, ". . . and there was not one feeble person among their tribes." Over two million people left Egypt during the exodus! One lamb served two purposes: salvation and healing.

The communion service has two elements: the cup and the wafer. The cup covers the forgiveness of sins. The wafer represents the broken body of Jesus, by Whose stripes we are healed. All who take communion are promised a double cure — forgiveness and healing — for double curse — sin and sickness.

In the hymn, "Rock of Ages," Augustus M. Toplady wrote this line: "Be of sin a double cure, save from wrath [salvation] and make me pure [whole]."

Not only is *therapeuo* a valid word for healing in the New Testament, its potency and vitality is still available today for all believers in Jesus Christ. Don't let theological rationalism or unbelief take from you the blessing of being healed in answer to believing prayer.

Not one verse of Scripture says answers to prayer were meant only for first century believers. Thank God, He still sends His Word and heals today as He did in the days of old. We serve a God Whose love, power and willingness to bless have never changed.

*I*n a sense the whole Bible is a revelation, not only of His willingness to heal our spiritual ailments, but our physical ones also. One of His covenant names is "The Lord that healeth" (Jehovah-*Rapha*), and He is also the Lord that changed not, the changeless, healing, health bestowing, life-giving Lord, undisputed Sovereign over all the powers of the universe.[1]

Lilian B. Yeomans, M.D.

2

Healing Scriptures

Old Testament

Genesis 20:17

So Abraham prayed to God; and God healed Abimelech, his wife, and his maid servants. Then they bore children.

NKJV

Exodus 15:26

And said, If thou wilt diligently hearken to the voice of the Lord thy God, and wilt do that which is right in his sight, and wilt give ear to his commandments, and keep all his statutes, I will put none of these diseases upon thee, which I have brought upon the Egyptians: for I am the Lord that healeth thee.

KJV

Here too, he gave them laws and decrees to live by, and issued this challenge to them: if thou wilt listen to the voice of the Lord thy God, his will doing, his word obeying, and all he bids thee observe, observing faithfully, never shall they fall on thee, the many woes brought on Egypt; I am the Lord, and it is health I bring thee.

Knox

Exodus 23:25,26

Worship the Lord your God, and his blessing will be on your food and water. I will take sickness from among you,

And none will miscarry or be barren in your land. I will give you a full life span.

NIV

Numbers 23:19

God is not a man, that he should lie, nor a son of man, that he should change his mind. Does he speak and then not act? Does he promise and not fulfill?

NIV

Deuteronomy 5:33

Ye shall walk in all the ways which the Lord your God hath commanded you, that ye may live, and that it may be well with you, and that ye may prolong your days in the land which ye shall possess.

KJV

Deuteronomy 7:11-15

Thou shalt therefore keep the commandments, and the statutes, and the judgments, which I command thee this day, to do them.

Wherefore it shall come to pass, if ye hearken to these judgments, and keep, and do them, that the Lord thy God shall keep unto thee the covenant and the mercy which he sware unto thy fathers:

And he will love thee, and bless thee, and multiply thee: he will also bless the fruit of thy womb, and the fruit of thy land, thy corn, and thy wine, and thine oil, the increase of thy kine, and the flocks of thy sheep, in the land which he sware unto thy fathers to give thee.

Thou shalt be blessed above all people: there shall not be male or female barren among you, or among your cattle.

And the Lord will take away from thee all sickness, and will put none of the evil diseases of Egypt, which thou knowest, upon thee; but will lay them upon all them that hate thee.

KJV

Deuteronomy 30:19,20

I call heaven and earth as witnesses today against you, *that* I have set before you life and death, blessing and cursing; therefore choose life, that both you and your descendants may live;

That you may love the Lord your God, that you may obey his voice, and that you may cling to him, for he is your life and the length of your days; and that you may dwell in the land which the Lord swore to your fathers, to Abraham, Isaac, and Jacob, to give them.

NKJV

Here and now I call heaven and earth to witness against you that I have put life and death before you, the blessing and the curse: choose life, then,

that you and your children may live, by loving the eternal your God, obeying his voice, and holding fast to him, for that means life to you and length of days, that you may live in the land which the eternal swore to Abraham, Isaac, and Jacob, your fathers, that he would give to them.

Moffatt

I call heaven and earth to witness this day that I have set such a choice before thee, life or death, a blessing or a curse. Wilt thou not choose life, long life for thyself and for those that come after thee?

Wilt thou not learn to love the Lord thy God, and obey him, and keep close to his side? Thou hast no life, no hope of long continuance, but in him; shall not the land which he promised as a gift to thy fathers, Abraham, Isaac and Jacob, be thine to dwell in?

Knox

1 Chronicles 28:28

And he (David) died in a good old age, full of days, riches, and honour.

KJV

2 Chronicles 16:9

For the eyes of the Lord run to and fro throughout the whole earth, to shew himself strong in the behalf of them whose heart is perfect toward him.

KJV

For the eternal's eyes dart here and there over the whole world, as he exerts his power on behalf of those who are devoted to him.

Moffatt

2 Chronicles 30:20

So the Lord heard Hezekiah and healed the people.

NAS

Job 5:26

Thou shalt come to thy grave in a full age, like as a shock of corn cometh in his season.

KJV

Job 37:23

Touching the almighty. . . *he* is excellent in power, and in judgment, and in plenty of justice: he will not afflict.

KJV

Psalm 30:2

O Lord my God, I cried unto thee, and thou hast healed me.

KJV

O Lord my God, I called to you for help and you healed me.

NIV

Psalm 30:2

I cried out to the Lord my God, and thou didst grant me recovery.

Knox

Psalm 34:19

Many are the afflictions of the righteous; but the Lord delivereth him out of them all.

KJV

Psalm 41:3

The Lord will strengthen him upon the bed of languishing: thou wilt make all his bed in his sickness.

KJV

The eternal sustains him on a sick bed, and brings him back to health.

Moffatt

The Lord will sustain, refresh, *and* strengthen him on his bed of languishing; all his bed you (O Lord) will turn, change *and* transform in his illness.

AMP

Psalm 91:10-16

There shall no evil befall you, nor any plague or calamity come near your tent.

For he will give his angels (especial) charge over you to accompany *and* defend *and* preserve you in all your ways (of obedience and service).

They shall bear you up on their hands, lest you dash your foot against a stone.

You shall tread upon the lion and adder; the young lion and the serpent shall you trample underfoot.

Because he has set his love upon me, therefore will I deliver him; I will set him on high because he knows and understands my name (has a personal knowledge of my mercy, love, and kindness, trusts and relies on me, knowing I will never forsake him, no never).

He shall call upon me and I will answer him; I will be with him in trouble, I will deliver him and honor him.

With long life will I satisfy him and show him my salvation.

AMP

Psalm 103:2,3

Bless the Lord, O my soul, and forget not all his benefits:

Who forgiveth all thine iniquities; who healeth all thy diseases.

KJV

Bless (affectionately, gratefully praise) the Lord, O my soul, and forget not (one of) all his benefits,

Who forgives (every one of) all your iniquities, who heals (each one of) all your diseases.

AMP

Bless the eternal, O my soul, remember all his benefits;

He pardons all your sins, and all your sicknesses he heals.

Moffatt

Psalm 105:37

He brought them forth also with silver and gold: and there was not one feeble person among their tribes.

KJV

Psalm 107:20

He sent his word, and healed them, and delivered them from their destructions.

KJV

He sent forth his word and healed them; he rescued *them* from the grave.

NIV

Psalm 147:3

He healeth the broken in heart, and bindeth up their wounds.

KJV

He heals the brokenhearted and binds up their wounds (curing their pains and their sorrows).

AMP

Proverbs 3:1,2

My son, do not forget my law,

But let your heart keep my commands; for length of days and long life and peace they will add to you.

NKJV

Proverbs 3:7,8

Do not be wise in your own eyes; fear the Lord and shun evil.

This will bring health to your body and nourishment to your bones.

NIV

Proverbs 4:20-22

My son, attend to my words; incline thine ear unto my sayings.

Let them not depart from thine eyes; keep them in the midst of thine heart.

For they are life unto those that find them and health to all their flesh.

KJV

Hear then and heed, my son, these words of warning;

Never lose sight of them, cherish them in thy inmost heart;

Let a man master them, they will bring life and healing to his whole being.

Knox

My son, attend to my words; consent *and* submit to my sayings.

Let them not depart from your sight; keep them in the center of your heart.

For they are life to those who find them, healing and health to all their flesh.

AMP

Proverbs 9:11

For by me thy days shall be multiplied, and the years of thy life shall be increased.

KJV

For through me your days will be many, and years will be added to your life.

NIV

Proverbs 14:30

A sound heart *is* the life of the flesh: but envy the rottenness of the bones.

KJV

Peace of mind is health of body; more than all else envy wastes the frame.

Knox

A *calm* and undisturbed mind *and* heart are the life *and* health of the body, but envy, jealousy, *and* wrath are like rottenness of the bones.

AMP

Proverbs 16:24

Pleasant words *are* as an honeycomb, sweet to the soul, and health to the bones.

KJV

Pleasant words are as a honeycomb, sweet to the mind and healing to the body.

AMP

Isaiah 40:29

He giveth power to the faint; and to t*hem that have* no might he increaseth strength.

KJV

Rather it is he who gives the weary fresh spirit, who fosters strength and vigour where strength and vigour is none.

Knox

Into the weary he puts power, and adds new strength to the weak.

Moffatt

Isaiah 40:31

But they that wait upon the Lord shall renew their strength; they shall mount up with wings as eagles; they shall run, and not be weary; *and* they shall walk, and not faint.

KJV

Isaiah 41:10

Fear thou not, for I am with thee; be not dismayed, for I *am* thy God, I will strengthen thee, yea, I will help thee, I will uphold thee with the right hand of my righteousness.

KJV

Fear not, for I am with you, I am your God, be not dismayed; I will strengthen, I will support you, I will uphold you with my trusty hand.

Moffatt

Have no fear, I am with thee; do not hesitate, am I not thy God? I am here to strengthen and protect thee; faithful the right hand that holds thee up.

Knox

Isaiah 53:4

Surely He has borne our griefs (sicknesses, weaknesses, and distresses) and carried our sorrows *and* pains (of punishment), yet we (ignorantly) considered Him stricken, smitten, and afflicted by God (as if with leprosy).

AMP

Isaiah 53:5

But he *was* wounded for our transgressions, *he was* bruised for our iniquities; the chastisement of our peace *was* upon him; and with his stripes we are healed.

KJV

Yet he was wounded because we had sinned, 'twas our misdeeds that crushed him; 'twas for our welfare that he was chastised, the blows that fell to him have brought us healing.

Moffatt

But he was wounded for our transgressions, he was bruised for our guilt *and* iniquities; the chastisement (needful to obtain) peace *and* well being for us was upon him, *and* with the stripes (that wounded) him we are healed *and* made whole.

AMP

Isaiah 55:11

So shall my word be that goeth forth out of my mouth: it shall not return unto me void, but it shall accomplish that which I please, and it shall prosper *in the thing* whereto I sent it.

KJV

So with the promise that has passed my lips; it falls not fruitless and in vain, but works out what I will, and carries out my purpose.

Moffatt

Isaiah 58:8

Then your light will break forth like the dawn, and your healing will quickly appear; then your righteousness will go before you, and the glory of the lord will be your rear guard.

NIV

Then shall your light break forth like the morning, and your healing (your restoration and the power of a new life) shall spring forth speedily; your righteousness (your rightness, your justice, and your right relationship with God) shall go before you (conducting you to peace and prosperity), and the glory of the Lord shall be your rear guard.

AMP

Jeremiah 17:14

Heal me, O Lord, and I will be healed: save me and I will be saved, for thou art my praise.

NAS

Malachi 4:2

But unto you who revere and worshipfully fear my name shall the Sun of righteousness arise with healing in his wings and his beams, and you shall go forth and gambol like calves (released) from the stall and leap for joy.

AMP

Malachi 3:6

For I am the Lord, I change not.

KJV

New Testament

Matthew 4:23,24

Jesus went throughout Galilee teaching in their synagogues, preaching the good news of the kingdom, and healing every disease and sickness among the people.

News about him spread all over Syria, and people brought to him all who were ill with various diseases, those suffering severe pain, the demon-possessed, those having seizures, and the paralyzed, and he healed them.

NIV

Matthew 6:9,10

After this manner therefore pray ye: Our Father which art in heaven, Hallowed be thy name.

Thy kingdom come. Thy will be done in earth, as *it is* in heaven.

KJV

Matthew 7:11

If ye then, being evil, know how to give good gifts unto your children, how much more shall your Father which is in heaven give good things to them that ask him?

KJV

Matthew 8:2,3

And a leper came to him, and throwing himself at his feet, said,

Sir if only you are willing you are able to cleanse me. So Jesus put out his hand and touched him, and said, "I am willing: Be cleansed." Instantly he was cleansed from his leprosy.

Weymouth

Matthew 8:5-10,13

As he entered Capernaum, a centurion came to him, asking for his aid;

Lord, he said, I have a servant lying sick at my house, cruelly tormented with the palsy.

Jesus said to him, I will come and heal him.

But the centurion answered, Lord, I am not worthy to receive thee under my roof; my servant will be healed if thou wilt only speak a word of command.

I too know what it is to obey authority; I have soldiers under me, and I say, Go, to one man, and he goes, or, Come, to another, and he comes, or, Do this, to my servant and he does it.

When he heard that, Jesus said to his followers in amazement, "Believe me, I have not found faith like this, even in Israel."

And to the centurion Jesus said, "Go then; let it be done to thee as thy faith foretold." And at that hour his servant was healed.

Knox

Matthew 8:14-17

And when Jesus went into Peter's house, He saw his mother-in-law lying ill with a fever.

He touched her hand and the fever left her; and she got up and began waiting on Him.

When evening came, they brought to Him many who were under the power of demons, and He drove out the spirits with a word and restored to health all who were sick.

And thus He fulfilled what was spoken by the prophet Isaiah, He Himself took (in order to carry away) our weaknesses and infirmities and bore away our diseases.

AMP

Matthew 9:20-22

And, behold, a woman, which was diseased with an issue of blood twelve years, came behind him, and touched the hem of his garment:

For she said within herself, If I may but touch his garment, I shall be whole.

But Jesus turned him about, and when he saw her, he said, Daughter, be of good comfort; thy faith hath made thee whole. And the woman was made whole from that hour.

KJV

And a woman who had a hemorrhage for twelve years came up and touched the tassel on His coat.

For she kept saying to herself, "If I can only touch His coat, I will get well."

And Jesus, on turning and seeing her, said, "Cheer up, my daughter! Your faith has cured you." And from that moment the woman was well.

Williams

Matthew 9:27-35

As Jesus was passing further on his way, he was followed by two blind men, who cried aloud, Son of David, have pity on us.

These blind men came to him when he had gone into his lodging, and Jesus said to them, Have you the faith to believe that I can do this? And they said to him, Yes, Lord.

Thereupon, he touched their eyes, and said, Your faith shall not be disappointed.

Then their eyes were opened; and Jesus laid a strict charge on them, telling them, Be sure nobody hears of this.

But they had no sooner gone out than they talked of him in all the country round.

And it chanced that, as they were going, a dumb man was brought to him, possessed with a devil.

The devil was cast out, and the dumb man found speech; at which the multitudes were filled with amazement; Nothing like this, they said, was ever seen in Israel.

But the Pharisees said, It is the prince of the devils that enables him to cast the devils out.

So Jesus went about all their cities and villages, teaching in their synagogues, preaching the Gospel of the kingdom, and curing every kind of disease and infirmity.

Knox

Matthew 10:1

And when he had called unto *him* his twelve disciples, he gave them power *against* unclean spirits, to cast them out, and to heal all manner of sickness and all manner of disease.

KJV

Matthew 10:7,8

And as ye go, preach, saying, The Kingdom of heaven is at hand.

Heal the sick, cleanse the lepers, raise the dead, cast out devils: freely ye have received, freely give.

KJV

Matthew 11:2-5

Now when John had heard in the prison the works of Christ, he sent two of his disciples,

And said unto him, Art thou he that should come, or do we look for another?

Jesus answered and said unto them, Go and shew John again those things which ye do hear and see:

The blind receive their sight, and the lame walk, the lepers are cleansed, and the deaf hear, the dead are raised up, and the poor have the gospel preached to them.

KJV

Matthew 12:15

But when Jesus knew it, he withdrew himself from thence: and great multitudes followed him, and he healed them all.

KJV

Matthew 14:13,14

When Jesus heard what had happened, he withdrew by boat privately to a solitary place. Hearing of this, the crowds followed him on foot from the towns.

When Jesus landed and saw a large crowd, he had compassion on them and healed their sick.

NIV

Matthew 14:34-36

When they had crossed over, they came to the land of Gennesaret.

And when the men of that place recognized Him, they sent out into all that surrounding region, brought to Him all who were sick,

and begged Him that they might only touch the hem of His garment. And as many as touched it were made perfectly well.

KJV

Matthew 15:29-31

Jesus left there and went along the Sea of Galilee. Then he went up on a mountainside and sat down.

Great crowds came to him, bringing the lame, the blind, and the crippled, the mute and many others, and laid them at his feet; and he healed them.

The people were amazed when they saw the mute speaking, the crippled made well, the lame walking and the blind seeing. And they praised the God of Israel.

NIV

Matthew 18:19

Again I say unto you, That if two of you shall agree on earth as touching any thing that they shall ask, It shall be done for them of my Father which is in heaven.

KJV

Again, I tell you, if only two of you on earth agree on what they pray for, they will get it from my Father in heaven.

Williams

Again I tell you, if two of you on earth agree (harmonize together, make a symphony together) about whatever (anything and everything) they may ask, it will come to pass *and* be done for them by My Father in heaven.

AMP

Matthew 19:1,2

And it came to pass, *that* when Jesus had finished these sayings, he departed from Galilee, and came into the coasts of Judea beyond Jordan;

And great multitudes followed him; and he healed them there.

KJV

Matthew 21:14

The blind and the lame came to him at the temple, and he healed them.

NIV

Matthew 24:35

Heaven and earth will pass away, but My words will by no means pass away.

NKJV

Matthew 13:58

And he did not many mighty works there because of their unbelief.

KJV

There he could not do many miracles owing to their lack of faith.

Moffatt

Mark 1:32-34

That evening after sunset the people brought to Jesus all the sick and demon possessed.

The whole town gathered at the door,

and Jesus healed many who had various diseases. He also drove out many demons, but he would not let the demons speak because they knew who he was.

NIV

Mark 2:1-12

And again he entered Capernaum after some days, and it was heard that He was in the house.

Immediately many gathered together, so that there was no longer room to receive *them,* not even near the door. And He preached the word to them.

Then they came to Him, bringing a paralytic who was carried by four men.

And when they could not come near Him because of the crowd, they uncovered the roof where He was. So when they had broken through, they let down the bed on which the paralytic was lying.

When Jesus saw their faith, He said to the paralytic, "Son, your sins are forgiven you."

And some of the scribes were sitting there and reasoning in their hearts,

"Why does this *man* speak blasphemies like this? Who can forgive sins but God alone?"

But immediately, when Jesus perceived in His spirit that they reasoned thus within themselves, he said to them, "Why do you reason about these things in your hearts?

Which is easier, to say to the paralytic, 'Your sins are forgiven you?' or to say, 'Arise, take up your bed and walk?' "

But that you may know that the Son of Man has power on earth to forgive sins — He said to the paralytic,

"I say to you, arise, take up your bed, and go to your house."

Immediately he arose, took up the bed, and went out in the presence of them all, so that all were amazed and glorified God, saying "We never saw anything like this!"

NKJV

Mark 3:10

For he had healed many; insomuch that they pressed upon him for to touch him, as many as had plagues.

KJV

Mark 5:21-43

When Jesus had again crossed over by boat to the other side of the lake, a large crowd gathered around him while he was by the lake.

Then one of the synagogue rulers, named Jairus, came there. Seeing Jesus he fell at his feet and pleaded earnestly with him, "My little daughter is dying. Please come and put your hands on her so that she will be healed and live."

So Jesus went with him. A large crowd followed and pressed around him.

And a woman was there who had been subject to bleeding for twelve years.

She had suffered a great deal under the care of many doctors and had spent all she had, yet instead of getting better she grew worse.

When she heard about Jesus, she came up behind him in the crowd and touched his cloak,

because she thought, "If I just touch his clothes, I will be healed."

Immediately her bleeding stopped and she felt in her body that she was freed from her suffering.

At once Jesus realized that power had gone out from him. He turned around in the crowd and asked, "Who touched my clothes?"

"You see the people crowding against you," his disciples answered, "and yet you can ask, "Who touched me?"

But Jesus kept looking around to see who had done it.

Then the woman, knowing what had happened to her, came and fell at his feet, and, trembling with fear, told him the whole truth.

He said to her, "Daughter, your faith has healed you. Go in peace and be freed from your suffering."

While Jesus was still speaking, some men came from the house of Jairus, the synagogue ruler. "Your daughter is dead," they said. "Why bother the teacher any more?"

Ignoring what they said, Jesus told the synagogue ruler, "Don't be afraid; just believe."

He did not let anyone follow him except Peter, James and John the brother of James.

When they came to the home of the synagogue ruler, Jesus saw a commotion, with people crying and wailing loudly.

He went in and said to them, "Why all this commotion and wailing? The child is not dead but asleep."

But they laughed at him. After he put them all out, he took the child's father and mother and the disciples who were with him, and went in where the child was.

He took her by the hand and said to her, "Talitha koum!" (which means, "Little girl, I say to you, get up!").

Immediately the girl stood up and walked around (she was twelve years old).

At this they were completely astonished. He gave strict orders not to let anyone know about this, and told them to give her something to eat.

NIV

Mark 6:5,6

And he could there do no mighty work, save that he laid his hands upon a few sick folk, and healed them.

And he marvelled because of their unbelief. And he went round about the villages, teaching.

KJV

He could not do any mighty deeds there, except that He put His hands on a few ailing people and cured them.

And He wondered at their lack of faith in Him.

Williams

Mark 6:53-56

When they had crossed over, they landed at Gennesaret, and moored the boat.

They had no sooner left her than the people recognizing Jesus,

hurried all over the country-side, and began to carry about upon mats those who were ill, wherever they heard he was.

So wherever he came — to villages, or towns, or farms — they would lay their sick in the marketplaces, and would beg him just to let them touch but the *tassel* of his *cloak;* and all who did so were made well.

Twentieth Century New Testament

Mark 10:46-52

Now they came to Jericho. As He went out of Jericho with His disciples and a great multitude, blind Bartimaeus, the son of Timaeus, sat by the road begging.

And when he heard that it was Jesus of Nazareth, he began to cry out and say, "Jesus, Son of David, has mercy on me!"

Then many warned him to be quiet; but he cried out all the more, "Son of David, have mercy on me!"

So Jesus stood still and commanded him to be called. Then they called the blind man, saying to him, "Be of good cheer, Rise, He is calling you."

And throwing aside his garment, he rose and came to Jesus.

So Jesus answered and said to him, "What do you want Me to do for you?" The blind man said to Him, "Rabboni, that I may receive my sight."

Then Jesus said to him, "Go your way; your faith has made you well." And immediately he received his sight and followed Jesus on the road.

NKJV

Mark 11:23,24

For verily I say unto you, That whosoever shall say unto this mountain, Be thou removed, and be thou cast into the sea; and shall not doubt in his heart, but shall believe that those things which he saith shall come to pass; he shall have whatsoever he saith.

Therefore I say unto you, What things so ever ye desire, when ye pray; believe that ye receive them, and ye shall have them.

KJV

I promise you, if anyone says to this mountain, Remove, and be cast into the sea, and has no hesitation in his heart, but is sure that what he says is to come about, his wish will be granted him.

I tell you, then, when you ask for anything in prayer, you have only to believe that it is yours, and it will be granted you.

Knox

Mark 16:15-20

And he said unto them, Go ye into all the world, and preach the gospel to every creature.

He that believeth and is baptized shall be saved; but he that believeth not shall be damned.

And these signs shall follow them that believe; In my name shall they cast out devils; they shall speak with new tongues;

They shall take up serpents; and if they drink any deadly thing, it shall not hurt them; they shall lay hands on the sick, and they shall recover.

So then after the Lord had spoken unto them, he was received up into heaven, and sat on the right hand of God.

And they went forth, and preached every where, the Lord working with *them*, and confirming the word with signs following. Amen.

KJV

Luke 4:16-21

And he came to Nazareth, where he had been brought up: and, as his custom was, he went into the synagogue on the sabbath day, and stood up for to read.

And there was delivered unto him the book of the prophet Esaias. And when he had opened the book, he found the place where it was written,

The Spirit of the Lord is upon me, because he hath anointed me to preach the gospel to the poor; he hath sent me to heal the brokenhearted, to preach deliverance to the captives, and recovering of sight to the blind, to set at liberty them that are bruised,

To preach the acceptable year of the Lord. And he closed the book, and he gave it again to the minister, and sat down.

And the eyes of all them that were in the synagogue were fastened on him.

And he began to say unto them, This day is this scripture fulfilled in your ears.

KJV

Luke 4:40

When the sun was setting, the people brought to Jesus all who had various kinds of sickness, and laying his hands on each one, he healed them.

NIV

Luke 6:6-10

And it came to pass also on another sabbath, that he entered into the synagogue and taught: and there was a man whose right hand was withered.

And the scribes and Pharisees watched him, whether he would heal on the sabbath day; that they might find an accusation against him.

But he knew their thoughts, and said to the man which had the withered hand, Rise up, and stand forth in the midst. And he arose and stood forth.

Then said Jesus unto them, I will ask you one thing; Is it lawful on the sabbath days to do good, or to do evil? to save life, or to destroy it?

And looking round about upon them all, he said unto the man, Stretch forth thy hand. And he did so, and his hand was restored whole as the other.

KJV

Luke 6:17-19

And he came down with them, and stood in the plain, and the company of his disciples, and a great multitude of people out of all Judea and Jerusalem, and from the sea coast of Tyre and Sidon, which came to hear him and to be healed of their diseases;

And they that were vexed with unclean spirits: and they were healed.

And the whole multitude sought to touch him: for there went virtue out of him and healed them all.

KJV

Afterward Jesus came down the hill with them and took his stand on a level place. With him were a large crowd of Judea, Jerusalem, and the coast district of Tyre and Sidon.

They had come to hear him and to be made well from their diseases.

Those, too, who were troubled with wicked spirits were cured;

And everybody in the crowd tried to touch him, because a power proceeded from him which made everyone well.

Twentieth Century New Testament

Luke 7:1-10

When Jesus had finished saying all this in the hearing of the people, he entered Capernaum.

There a centurion's servant, whom his master valued highly, was sick and about to die.

The centurion heard of Jesus and sent some elders of the Jews to him, asking him to come and heal his servant.

When they came to Jesus, they pleaded earnestly with him. "This man deserves to have you do this,

Because he loves our nation and has built our synagogue."

So Jesus went with them. He was not far from the house when the centurion sent friends to say to him: "Lord, don't trouble yourself, for I do not deserve to have you come under my roof.

That is why I did not even consider myself worthy to come to you. But say the word, and my servant will be healed.

For I myself am a man under authority, with soldiers under me. I tell this one, 'Go,' and he goes; and that one, 'Come,' and he comes. I say to my servant, 'Do this,' and he does it."

When Jesus heard this, he was amazed at him, and turning to the crowd following him, he said, "I tell you, I have not found such great faith even in Israel."

Then the men who had been sent returned to the house and found the servant well.

NIV

Luke 9:1,2,6,11

Then he called his twelve disciples together, and gave them power and authority over all devils, and to cure diseases.

And he sent them to preach the kingdom of God, and to heal the sick.

And they departed, and went through the towns, preaching the gospel and healing every where.

And the people, when they knew *it,* followed him: and he received them, and spake unto them of the kingdom of God, and healed them that had need of healing.

KJV

Luke 10:8,9

And into whatsoever city ye enter, and they receive you, eat such things as are set before you:

And heal the sick that are therein, and say unto them, The kingdom of God is come nigh unto you.

KJV

Luke 7:11-19

And it came to pass, as he went to Jerusalem, that he passed through the midst of Samaria and Galilee.

And as he entered into a certain village, there met him ten men that were lepers, which stood afar off:

And they lifted up their voices, and said, Jesus, Master, have mercy on us.

And when he saw them, he said unto them, Go shew your selves unto the priests. And it came to pass, that as they went, they were cleansed.

And one of them, when he saw that he was healed, turned back, and with a loud voice glorified God,

And fell down on *his* face at his feet, giving him thanks: and he was a Samaritan.

And Jesus answering said, Were there not ten cleansed? but where are the nine?

There are not found that returned to give glory to God, save this stranger.

And he said unto him arise, go thy way; thy faith hath made thee whole.

KJV

Luke 18:35-43

As Jesus approached Jericho, a blind man was sitting by the roadside begging.

When he heard the crowd going by, he asked what was happening.

They told him, "Jesus of Nazareth is passing by."

He called out, "Jesus, Son of David, have mercy on me!"

Those who led the way rebuked him and told him to be quiet, but he shouted all the more, "Son of David, have mercy of me!"

Jesus stopped and ordered the man to be brought to him. When he came near, Jesus asked him, "What do you want me to do for you?"

"Lord, I want to see," he replied.

Jesus said to him, " Receive your sight; your faith has healed you."

Immediately he received his sight and followed Jesus, praising God. When all the people saw it, they also praised God.

NIV

John 5:2-14

Now there is at Jerusalem by the sheep *market* a pool, which is called in the Hebrew tongue Bethesda, having five porches.

In these lay a great multitude of impotent folk, of blind, halt, withered, waiting for the moving of the water.

For an angel went down at a certain season into the pool, and troubled the water: whosoever then first after the troubling of the water stepped in was made whole of whatsoever disease he had.

And a certain man was there, which had an infirmity thirty and eight years.

When Jesus saw him lie, and knew that he had been now a long time *in that case*, he saith unto him, Wilt thou be made whole?

The impotent man answered him, Sir, I have no man, when the water is troubled, to put me into the pool: but while I am coming, another steppeth down before me.

Jesus saith unto him, Rise, take up thy bed, and walk.

And immediately the man was made whole, and took up his bed, and walked: and on the same day was the sabbath.

The Jews therefore said unto him that was cured, It is the sabbath day: it is not lawful for thee to carry *thy* bed.

He answered them, He that made me whole, the same said unto me, Take up thy bed, and walk.

Then asked they him, What man is that which said unto thee, Take up thy bed, and walk?

And he that was healed wist not who it was: for Jesus had conveyed himself away, a multitude being in *that* place.

Afterward Jesus findeth him in the temple, and said unto him, Behold, thou art made whole: sin no more, lest a worse thing come unto thee.

KJV

John 9:1-7

Now as Jesus passed by, He saw a man who was blind from birth.

And His disciples asked Him, saying, "Rabbi, who sinned, this man or his parents, that he was born blind?"

Jesus answered, "Neither this man nor this parents sinned; but that the works of God should be revealed in him.

I must work the works of Him who sent Me while it is day; the night is coming when no one can work.

As long as I am in the world I am the light of the world."

When He had said these things, He spat on the ground and made clay with the saliva; and He anointed the eyes of the blind man with the clay.

And He said to him, "Go, wash in the pool of Siloam" (which is translated, Sent). So he went and washed, and came back seeing.

NKJV

John 10:10

The thief cometh not, but for to steal, and to kill, and to destroy: I am come that they might have life, and that they might have *it* more abundantly.

KJV

A thief does not come for any purpose but to steal and kill and destroy; I have come for people to have life and have it till it overflows.

Williams

John 14:13,14

And whatsoever ye shall ask in my name, that will I do, that the Father may be glorified in the Son.

If ye shall ask any thing in my name, I will do *it*.

KJV

John 15:7

If you remain in union with me and my words remain in you, you may ask whatever you please and you shall have it.

Williams

John 16:23,24

And in that day ye shall ask me nothing. Verily, verily, I say unto you, Whatsoever ye shall ask the Father in my name, he will give it to you.

Hitherto have ye asked nothing in my name: ask and ye shall receive, that your joy may be full.

KJV

When that day comes, you will not need to ask anything of me. Believe me, you have only to make any request of the Father in my name, and he will grant it to you.

Until now, you have not been making any requests in my name; make them, and they will be granted, to bring your gladness in full measure.

Knox

Acts 5:12

And by the hands of the apostles were many signs and wonders wrought among the people.

KJV

Acts 5:16

There came also a multitude *out* of the cities round about unto Jerusalem, bringing sick folks, and them which were vexed with unclean spirits: and they were healed every one.

KJV

Acts 3:1-8

One day Peter and John were going up to the temple at the time of prayer — at three in the afternoon.

Now a man crippled from birth was being carried to the temple gate called Beautiful, where he was put every day to beg from those going into the temple courts.

When he saw Peter and John about to enter, he asked them for money.

Peter looked straight at him, as did John. Then Peter said, "Look at us!"

So the man gave them his attention, expecting to get something from them.

Then Peter said, "Silver or gold I do not have, but what I have I give you. In the name of Jesus Christ of Nazareth, walk."

Taking him by the right hand, he helped him up, and instantly the man's feet and ankles became strong.

He jumped to his feet and began to walk. Then he went with them into the temple courts, walking and jumping, and praising God.

NIV

Acts 8:5-8

Then Philip went down to the city of Samaria and preached Christ to them.

And the multitudes with one accord heeded the things spoken by Philip, hearing and seeing the miracles which he did.

For unclean spirits, crying with a loud voice, came out of many who were possessed; and many who were paralyzed and lame were healed.

And there was great joy in that city.

NKJV

Acts 9:33,34

There he found a man called Aeneas, who had not left his bed for eight years, being palsied.

And Peter said to him, Aeneas, Jesus Christ sends thee healing; rise up, and make thy bed; whereupon he rose up at once.

Knox

Acts 10:38

How God anointed Jesus of Nazareth with the Holy Ghost and with power: who went about doing good, and healing all that were oppressed of the devil; for God was with him.

KJV

Acts 14:8-10

Now a man who had no power in his feet used to sit in the streets of Lystra. He had been lame from his birth and had never walked.

After this man had listened to one of Paul's sermons, the Apostle, looking steadily at him and perceiving that he had faith to be cured, said in a loud voice,

"Stand upright upon your feet!"

Weymouth

Acts 19:11,12

And God wrought special miracles by the hands of Paul:

So that from his body were brought unto the sick handkerchiefs or aprons, and the diseases departed from them, and the evil spirits went out of them.

KJV

Romans 4:19-21

And being not weak in faith, he considered not his own body now dead, when he was about an hundred years old, neither yet the deadness of Sarah's womb:

He staggered not at the promise of God through unbelief; but was strong in faith, giving glory to God;

And being fully persuaded that, what he had promised, he was able also to perform.

KJV

His faith never quailed, even when he noted the utter impotence of his own body (for he was about a hundred years old) or the impotence of Sara's womb;

No unbelief made him waver about God's promise;

His faith won strength as he gave glory to God and felt convinced that He was able to do what He had promised.

Moffatt

Romans 8:32

Since He did not spare His own Son but gave Him up for us all, will he not with Him graciously give us everything else?

Williams

Romans 8:11

But if the Spirit of Him who raised Jesus from the dead dwells in you, He who raised Christ from the dead will also give life to your mortal bodies through His Spirit who dwells in you.

NKJV

So then faith cometh by hearing, and hearing by the word of God.

KJV

1 Corinthians 6:20

For ye are bought with a price: therefore glorify God in your body and in your spirit, which are God's.

KJV

1 Corinthians 12:7-11,28

But the manifestation of the Spirit is given to every man to profit withal.

For to one is given by the Spirit the word of wisdom; to another the word of knowledge by the same Spirit;

To another faith by the same Spirit; to another the gifts of healing by the same Spirit;

To another the working of miracles; to another prophecy; to another discerning of spirits; to another *divers* kinds of tongues; to another the interpretation of tongues;

But all these worketh that one and the selfsame Spirit, dividing to every man severally as he will.

And God hath set some in the church, first apostles, secondarily prophets, thirdly teachers, after that miracles, then gifts of healing, helps, governments, diversities of tongues.

KJV

Galatians 3:13,14

Christ redeemed us from the curse of the law by becoming a curse for us, for it is written: Cursed is everyone who is hung on a tree.

That the blessing given to Abraham might come on the Gentiles through Christ Jesus; that we might receive the promise of the Spirit through faith.

KJV

Ephesians 5:30

For we are members of his body, of his flesh, and of his bones.

KJV

Ephesians 6:1-3

Children be obedient to your parents as a Christian duty, for it is a duty.

"Honour your father and your mother" this is the first Commandment which has a promise added to it

"so that it may be well with you, and that you may live long on the earth."

Weymouth

Philippians 2:8-11

And being found in fashion as a man, he humbled himself, and became obedient unto death, even the death of the cross.

Wherefore God also hath highly exalted him, and given him a name which is above every name:

That at the name of Jesus every knee should bow, of *things* in heaven, and *things* in earth, and *things* under the earth;

And that every tongue should confess that Jesus Christ is Lord, to the glory of God the Father.

KJV

Then he appeared among us as a man, and still further humbled himself by submitting even to death — yes, death on a cross!

And this is why God raised him to the very highest place, and gave him the Name which ranks above all others,

So that in honour of the Name of Jesus every *knee should bend*, in Heaven, on earth, and under the earth,

And that *every tongue should acknowledge* Jesus Christ as Lord — to the glory of God the Father.

Twentieth Century New Testament

1 Thessalonians 5:23

And the very God of peace sanctify you wholly; and *I pray God* your whole spirit and soul and body be preserved blameless unto the coming of our Lord Jesus Christ.

KJV

May the God of peace consecrate you through and through! Spirit, soul, and body, may you be kept without break or blame till the arrival of our Lord Jesus Christ!

Moffatt

So may the God of peace sanctify you wholly, keep spirit and soul and body unimpaired, to greet the coming of our Lord Jesus Christ without reproach.

Knox

2 Timothy 1:7

For God hath not given us the spirit of fear; but of power, and of love, and of a sound mind.

KJV

For God did not give us a spirit of timidity (of cowardice, of craven and cringing and fawning fear), but (he has given us a spirit) of power and of love and of calm and well-balanced mind and discipline and self-control.

AMP

Hebrews 2:14,15

Forasmuch then as the children are partakers of flesh and blood, he also himself likewise took part of the same;

that through death he might destroy him that had the power of death, that is, the devil;

And deliver them who through fear of death were all their lifetime subject to bondage.

KJV

Since then the children referred to are all alike sharers in perishable human nature, He Himself also, in the same way, took on Him a share of it, in order that through death He might render powerless him who had authority over death, that is, the Devil,

and might set at liberty all those who through fear of death had been subject to lifelong slavery.

Weymouth

Hebrews 4:14-16

Inasmuch then as we have a great High Priest who has (already) ascended *and* passed through the heavens, Jesus the Son of God, let us hold fast our confession (of faith in Him).

For we do not have a High Priest Who is unable to understand *and* sympathize *and* have a shared feeling with our weaknesses *and* infirmities *and* liability to the assaults of temptation, but One who has been tempted in every respect as we are, yet without sinning.

Let us then fearlessly *and* confidently *and* boldly draw near to the throne of grace (the throne of God's unmerited favor to us sinners), that we may receive mercy (for our failures) and find grace to help in good time for every need (appropriate help and well-timed help, coming just when we need it).

AMP

Hebrews 10:23

Let us hold fast the profession of our faith without wavering; (for he *is* faithful that promised).

KJV

Let us, without ever wavering, keep on holding to the hope that we profess, for He is to be trusted who has made the promise.

Williams

Hebrews 10:35,36

Cast now away therefore your confidence, which hath great recompense of reward.

For ye have need of patience, that, after ye have done the will of God, ye might receive the promise.

KJV

Now do not drop that confidence of yours; it carries with it a rich hope of reward.

Steady patience is what you need, so that after doing the will of God you may receive what you were promised.

Moffatt

Hebrews 11:1

Now faith is being sure of what we hope for and certain of what we do not see. This is what the ancients were commended for.

NIV

Now faith is a well-grounded assurance of that for which we hope, and a conviction of the reality of things which we do not see.

Weymouth

What is faith? It is that which give substance to our hopes, which convinces us of things we cannot see.

Knox

Hebrews 11:6

But without faith *it is* impossible to please *him:* for he that cometh to God must believe *that* he is, and that he is a rewarder of them that diligently seek him.

KJV

Hebrews 13:8

Jesus Christ *is* the same yesterday and today, *yes* and forever.

NAS

James 1:17

Whatever gifts are worth having, whatever endowments are perfect of their kind, these come to us from above; they are sent down by the Father of all that gives light, with whom there can be no change, no swerving from his course.

Knox

James 5:14-16

Is anyone sick among you? He should call in the elders of the church, and they should pray over him, and anoint him with oil in the name of the Lord,

and the prayer that is offered in faith will save the sick man; the Lord will raise him to health, and if he has committed sins, he will be forgiven.

So practice confessing your sins to one another, and praying for one another, that you may be cured. An upright man's prayer, when it keeps at work, is very powerful.

Williams

1 Peter 2:24

Who his own self bare our sins in his own body on the tree, that we, being dead to sins, should live unto righteousness: by whose stripes ye were healed.

KJV

He personally bore our sins in His (own) body on the tree as on an altar and offered Himself (on it), that we might die (cease to exist) to sin and live to righteousness. By His wounds you have been healed.

AMP

The burden of our sins He Himself carried in his own body to the Cross and bore it there, so that we, having died so far as our sins are concerned, may live righteous lives. By His wounds yours have been healed.

Weymouth

1 John 5:14,15

Now this is the confidence that we have in Him, that if we ask anything according to His will, He hears us.

And if we know that He hears us, whatever we ask, we know that we have the petitions that we have asked of Him.

NKJV

Such familiar confidence we have in him, that we believe he listens to us whenever we make any request of him in accordance with his will.

We are sure that he listens to all our requests, sure that the requests we make of him are granted.

Knox

3 John 2

My dear friend, I pray that you may in all respects prosper and enjoy good health, just as your soul already prospers.

Weymouth

*J*esus came to deliver men from sin and sickness that He might make known the love of the Father. In his actions, in his teachings of the disciples and in the work of the apostles, pardon and healing are always found together.[2]

Andrew Murray

3

The Healings of Christ

Jesus began His public ministry as a ministry of miracles. Everything about His life involved miracles: His conception, birth, life, wisdom and teachings, ministry, death, resurrection, appearances, and ascension — all of these were astounding and undeniable miracles.

Many people have said that miracles were just for the days of the Old and New Testaments, but that is not true. Jesus Christ is as much a miracle-worker now as He ever was; and people need His miracle touch now more than ever.

We are called to walk as the Christians did in the New Testament. To serve the needs of people today, Jesus must be allowed to live in us, in His power and with His personal presence guiding us. This is true Christianity — walking in the power and presence and wisdom of Jesus. So many religious ceremonies are merely impersonal tradition, offering nothing but a lifeless formality. Jesus' ministry brought life and deliverance everywhere He went. He wants us to live aware of His loving, miracle-working power.

When people act on God's Word in bold faith, the faith which produces miracles, then multitudes will come from miles, eager to see Christ's miracle-power in demonstration.

Jesus always attracted the multitudes by His miracles then and He does so today, wherever miracles are done in His name. He is the same yesterday, today and forever.

If we preach as the early Church preached, we will get the same results that they got: miracles and healings. It doesn't matter where we are or who we are. If we want to get Bible results, we have to preach what the Bible says: that miracles are a part of the present-day ministry of Jesus Christ.

The Healings of Christ

	Matthew	Mark	Luke	John
1. Nobleman's son healed				4:46-54
2. Healing the demoniac		1:23-28	4:33-37	
3. Healing Peter's mother-in-law	8:14-15	1:29-31	4:38-39	
4. Healing of the leper	8:2-4	1:40-42	5:12-13	
5. Healing the paralytic	9:2-8	2:2-12	5:18-26	
6. Healing the man at the pool				5:2-9
7. Healing the withered hand	12:9-13	3:1-5	6:6-10	
8. Healing many near Galilee	12:15	3:7-12		
9. Healing the centurion's servant	8:5-13		7:2-10	

4

Seven Ways Jesus Healed

1. Jesus Healed by Speaking the Word

And it came to pass, as he went to Jerusalem, that he passed through the midst of Samaria and Galilee.

And as he entered into a certain village, there met him ten men that were lepers, which stood afar off:

And they lifted up their voices, and said, Jesus, Master, have mercy on us.

And when he saw them, he said unto the, Go shew your selves unto the priests. And it came to pass, that as they went, they were cleansed.

And one of them, when he saw that he was healed, turned back, and with a loud voice glorified God,

And fell down on his face at his feet, giving him thanks: and he was a Samaritan.

And Jesus answering said, Were there not ten cleansed? but where are the nine?

There are not found that returned to give glory to God, save this stranger.

And he said unto him, Arise, go thy way: thy faith hath made thee whole.

Luke 17:11-19

Here is a case in which Jesus just spoke a word or gave instructions and the recipients received their healing. Jesus said in Matthew 7:24 *"those who heareth these sayings of mine, and doeth them, I will liken him unto as a wise man."* Jesus healed with His Word.

2. Jesus Healed by Laying Hands on or Touching the Sick

And as they departed from Jericho, a great multitude followed him.

And, behold, two blind men sitting by the way side, when they heard that Jesus passed by, cried out, saying, Have mercy on us, O Lord, *thou* son of David.

And the multitude rebuked them, because they should hold their peace: but they cried the more, saying, Have mercy on us, O Lord, *thou* son of David.

And Jesus stood still, and called them, and said, What will ye that I shall do unto you?

They say unto him, Lord, that our eyes may be opened.

So Jesus had compassion on them, and touched their eyes: and immediately their eyes received sight, and they followed him.

Matthew 20:29-34

And there came a leper to him, beseeching him, and kneeling down to him, and saying unto him, If thou wilt, thou canst make me clean.

And Jesus, moved with compassion, put forth his hand, and touched him, and saith unto him, I will; be thou clean.

And as soon as he had spoken, immediately the leprosy departed from him, and he was cleansed.

Mark 1:40-42

Now when the sun was setting all they that had any sick with divers diseases brought them unto him; and he laid his hands on every one of them, and healed them.

Luke 4:40

And when Jesus saw her, he called her to him, and said unto her, Woman, thou art loosed form thine infirmity.

And he laid his hands on her: and immediately she was made straight, and glorified God.

Luke 13:12,13

These Scriptures show that Jesus healed by touching or laying His hands upon the sick. Likewise, Jesus left believers with the commission to *". . .lay hands on the sick, and they shall recover"* (Mark 16:18). Jesus healed by laying hands on the sick.

3. Jesus Healed Through the Virtue or Power That Was Accessible in Him

And when they were gone over, they came into the land of Gennesaret.

And when the men of that place had knowledge of him, they sent out into all that country round about, and brought unto him all that were diseased;

And besought him that they might only touch the hem of his garment; and as many as touched were made perfectly whole.

Matthew 14:34-36

For he had healed many insomuch that they pressed upon him for to touch him, as many as had plagues.

Mark 3:10

And a certain woman, which had an issue of blood twelve years,

And had suffered many things of many physicians, and had spent all that she had, and was nothing bettered, but rather grew worse,

When she had heard of Jesus, came in the press behind, and touched his garment.

For she said, If I may touch but his clothes, I shall be whole.

And straightway the fountain of her blood was dried up; and she felt in *her* body that she was healed of that plague.

And Jesus, immediately knowing in himself that virtue had gone out of him, turned him about in the press, and said, Who touched my clothes?

And his disciples said unto him, Thou seest the multitude thronging thee, and sayest thou, Who touched me?

And he looked round about to see her that had done this thing.

But the woman fearing and trembling, knowing what was done in her, came and fell down before him and told him all the truth.

And he said unto her, Daughter, thy faith hath made thee whole; go in peace, and be whole of thy plague.

Mark 5:25-34

And ran through that whole region round about, and began to carry about in beds those that were sick, where they heard he was.

And whithersoever he entered, into villages, or cities, or country, they laid the sick in the streets, and besought him that they might touch if it were but the border of his garment: and as many as touched him were made whole.

Mark 6:55,56

And the whole multitude sought to touch him: for there went virtue out him, and healed them all.

Luke 6:19

These passages of Scripture relate how individuals reached out in faith and touched the garment Jesus was wearing. They were made perfectly whole. The combination of God's healing power operating in Jesus, mixed with the faith of the individual in need, brought about the healing of their body. That same healing power or virtue still flows out from Christ today. It is still received by faith.

4. Jesus Healed Through the Faith of Others

And when Jesus entered into Capernaum, there came unto him a centurion, beseeching him,

And saying, Lord, my servant lieth at home sick of the palsy, grievously tormented.

And Jesus saith unto him, I will come and heal him.

The centurion answered and said, Lord, I am not worthy that thou shouldest come under my roof: but speak the word only and my servant shall be healed.

For I am a man under authority, having soldiers under me: and I say to this *man*, Go, and he goeth: and to another, Come, and he cometh; and to my servant, Do this, and he doeth it.

When Jesus heard it, he marvelled, and said to them that followed, Verily I say unto you, I have not found so great faith no, not in Israel.

And I say unto you, That many shall come from the east and west, and shall sit down with Abraham, and Isaac, and Jacob, in the kingdom of heaven.

But the children of the kingdom shall be cast out into outer darkness: there shall be weeping and gnashing of teeth.

And Jesus said unto the centurion, Go thy way; and as thou hast believed, so be it done unto thee. And his servant was healed in the selfsame hour.

Matthew 8:5-13

And when Jesus was passed over again by ship unto the other side, much people gathered unto him: and he was nigh unto the sea.

And, behold, there cometh one of the rulers of the synagogue, Jairus by name; and when he saw him, he fell at his feet,

And besought him greatly, saying, My little daughter lieth at the point of death: *I pray thee*, come and lay thy hands on her, that she may be healed; and she shall live.

And he took the damsel by the hand, and said unto her, Talitha cumi; which is being interpreted, Damsel, I say unto thee, arise.

And straightway the damsel arose, and walked; for she was of the age of twelve years. And they were astonished with great astonishment.

Mark 5:21-23; 41,42

And behold, men brought in a bed a man which was taken with a palsy: and they sought *means* to bring *him* in, and to lay him before him.

And when they could not find by what way they might bring him in because of the multitude, they went upon the housetop, and let him down through the tiling with *his* couch into the midst before Jesus.

And when he saw their faith, he said unto him, Man, thy sins are forgiven thee.

And the scribes and the Pharisees began to reason, saying, Who is this which speaketh blasphemies? Who can forgive sins, but God alone?

But when Jesus perceived their thoughts, he answering said unto them, What reason ye in your hearts?

Whether is easier, to say, Thy sins be forgiven thee; or to say, Rise up and walk?

But that ye may know that the Son of man hath power upon earth to forgive sins, (he said unto the sick of the palsy,) I say unto thee, Arise, and take up thy couch, and go into thine house.

And immediately he rose up before them, and took up that whereon he lay, and departed to his own house, glorifying God.

Luke 5:18-25

In these healing examples, people request healing for someone else. They came to Jesus in faith on behalf of another person who was too sick or unable to believe for himself. Today we can go to our Heavenly Father in Jesus' name and intercede on behalf of those who need a healing touch.

5. Jesus Healed Through the Gifts of Healing

After this there was a feast of the Jews; and Jesus went up to Jerusalem.

Now there is at Jerusalem by the sheep *market* a pool, which is called in the Hebrew tongue Bethesda, having five porches.

In these lay a great multitude of impotent folk, of blind, halt, withered, waiting for the moving of the water.

For an angel went down at a certain season into the pool, and troubled the water: whosoever then first after the troubling of the water stepped in was made whole of whatsoever disease he had.

And a certain man was there, which had an infirmity thirty and eight years.

When Jesus saw him lie, and knew that he had been now a long time *in that case*, he saith unto him, Wilt thou be made whole?

The impotent man answered him, Sir, I have no man, when the water is troubled, to put me into the pool: but while I am coming, another steppeth down before me.

Jesus saith unto him, Rise, take up thy bed, and walk.

And immediately the man was made whole, and took up his bed, and walked: and on the same day was the sabbath.

John 5:1-9

During His earthly ministry, Jesus operated in all of the gifts of the Spirit. This is an instance when Jesus did not lay hands on the man and he was not releasing any faith for his healing. Jesus simply healed this man. This is how the gifts of healing operate. The manifestation of the gifts of healing are totally dependent and operate as the Spirit wills, not by the will of man.

6. Jesus Healed Through Unorthodox Means

And he cometh to Bethsaida: and they bring a blind man unto him, and besought him to touch him.

And he took the blind man by the hand, and led him out of the town; and when had spit on his eyes, and put his hands upon him, he asked him if he saw ought.

And he looked up, and said, I see men as trees, walking.

After that he put *his* hands again upon his eyes, and made him look up: and he was restored, and saw every man clearly.

Mark 8:22-25

And as *Jesus* passed by, he saw a man which was blind from his birth.

And his disciples asked him, saying, Master, who did sin, this man, or his parents, that he was born blind?

Jesus answered, Neither hath this man sinned, nor his parents: but that the works of God might be made manifest in Him.

I must work the works of him that sent me while it is day: the night cometh, when no man can work.

As long as I am in the world, I am the light of the world.

When he had thus spoken, he spat on the ground, and made clay of the spittle, and he anointed the eyes of the blind man with the clay,

And said unto him, Go, wash in the pool of Siloam, (which is by interpretation, Sent.) He went his way therefore, and washed, and came seeing.

John 9:1-7

Jesus healed two men in very unusual ways. Whether the manner in which He healed was unusual or not, the men received their sight.

7. Jesus Healed Through Empowering His Disciples

And when he had called unto him his twelve disciples, he gave them power against unclean spirits, to cast them out, and to heal all manner of sickness and all manner of disease.

Matthew 10:1

And he called *unto him* the twelve, and began to send them forth by two and two; and gave them power over unclean spirits;

and commanded them that they should take nothing for *their* journey, save a staff only; no scrip, no bread, no money in *their* purse:

But *be* shod with sandals; and not put on two coats.

And he said unto them, In what place soever ye enter into an house, there abide till ye depart from that place.

And whosoever shall not receive you, nor hear you, when ye depart thence, shake off the dust under your feet for a testimony against them. Verily I say unto you, It shall be more tolerable for Sodom and Gomorrha in the day of judgement than for that city.

And they went out, and preached that men should repent.

And they cast out many devils, and anointed with oil many that were sick, and healed them.

Mark 6:7-13

Then he called his twelve disciples together, and gave them power and authority over all devils, and to cure diseases.

And he sent them to preach the kingdom of God, and to heal the sick.

Luke 9:1,2

After these things the Lord appointed other seventy also, and sent them two and two before his face into every city and place, wither he himself would come.

And into whatsoever city ye enter, and they receive you, eat such things as are set before you:

And heal the sick that are therein, and say unto them, The kingdom of God is come nigh unto you.

Luke 10:1, 8,9

Jesus commissioned His disciples to go forth and to duplicate His work. They were called to preach the Gospel of the kingdom and to heal the sick. The Lord Jesus has given us all that same commission to *"preach the gospel to every creature"* and to *"lay hands on the sick."* (Mark 16:15-18.)

These are only seven ways Jesus healed during His ministry on the earth. There are possibly many other ways

Jesus healed the sick, for the Bible says that there were many other things Jesus did and if all were written down, the world could not contain the books. (John 21:25.) The good news for believers today is: God is still in the healing business and Jesus is still the healer. *"Jesus Christ the same yesterday, and today and forever."* (Hebrews 13:8).

If you are sick, put yourself in contact with God's law of life. Read His Word with a view of enlightening your heart so that you will be able to look up with more confidence and believe Him. Pray that the Spirit of God will come into your soul, take possession of your body, and its power will make you well. That is the exercise of the law of the spirit of life in Christ Jesus.[3]

John G. Lake

5

One Hundred Divine Healing Facts

1. Sickness is no more natural than sin. God made all things *very good*. (Gen. 1:31.) Therefore, we should not look for the remedy of sin or sickness in the natural, but from God who created us happy, strong, healthy, and to fellowship with Him.

2. Both sin and sickness came into the world through the fall of the human race. Therefore, we must look for the healing of both in the savior of the human race.

3. When God called His children out of Egypt, He made a covenant of healing with them. (Ex. 15:26; 23:25.) Throughout history, we find them in sickness and in pestilence, turning to God in repentance and confession; and, always, when their sins were forgiven, their sicknesses were healed.

4. God healed those who were bitten by fiery serpents as they looked at a brazen serpent on a pole, which is a type of Calvary. (Num. 21:8.) If everyone who looked at the brazen serpent was healed then, it is logical that everyone who looks at Jesus now can be healed.

5. Jesus said: *As Moses lifted up the serpent in the wilderness, even so* (for the same purpose) *must the Son of man be lifted up.* (John 3:14-15, Num. 21:4-9.)

6. The people had sinned against God then. Humankind has sinned against God today.

7. The poisonous serpent's bite resulted in death then. Sin results in death today. (Rom. 6:23).

8. The people cried to God then, and He heard their cry and provided a remedy — the *serpent lifted up*. Those who cry to God today discover that God has heard their cry and has provided them a remedy — *Christ lifted up*.

9. The remedy was for *everyone that is bitten* then. The remedy is for *whoever believes* today.

10. In their remedy they received both forgiveness for their sins and healing for their bodies. In Christ, we receive both forgiveness for our sins and healing for our bodies.

11. There were no exceptions then -- their remedy was for *everyone that was bitten*. There are no exceptions today — our remedy is for *whoever believes*.

12. Everyone was commanded to individually look at the remedy then. Everyone is commanded to individually believe on Christ today.

13. They did not need to beg nor make an offering to God then. There was only one condition: *When they look*. We do not need to beg nor make an offering to Christ today. There is only one condition: *Whoever believes*.

14. They were not told to look to Moses, but rather to the remedy then. We are not told to look to the preacher, but to Christ today.

15. They were not to look to the symptoms of their snakebites then, but rather to their remedy. We are not to look to the symptoms of our sins and diseases today, but to our remedy, Christ.

16. *Everyone that is bitten, when he or she looks upon it, shall live* was the promise to all then, without exception. *Whoever believes in him should not perish, but have everlasting life* is the promise to all today, without exception.

17. Since their curse was removed by the lifting up of the "type" of Christ, our curse was certainly removed by Christ Himself. (Gal. 3:13.)

18. The "type" of Christ could not mean more than to those Israelites, than Christ means to us today. Surely they, through only a "type" of Christ, could not receive more blessings which we cannot receive today through Christ Himself.

19. God promises protection for our bodies as well as for our spirits, if we live in Him. (Ps. 91). In the New Testament, John wishes *above all things that you may prosper and be in health, even as your soul prospers.* (3 John. 2.) Both Scriptures show that God's will is that we be as healthy in our bodies as we are in our spirits. It is never God's will for our spirits to be sick. It is never God's will for our bodies to be sick.

20. Asa died in his sickness because he *sought not the Lord, but to the physicians;* (2 Chron. 16) while Hezekiah lived because he sought not to the physicians, but to the Lord. (Isa. 38.)

21. The removal of our diseases is included in Christ's redemptive work, along with the removal of our sins. (Isa. 53). The word "bore" implies substitution (suffering for), no sympathy (suffering with). If Christ has borne our sicknesses, why should we bear them?

22. Christ fulfilled Isaiah's words: *He healed all that were sick.* (Mt. 8:16,17.)

23. Sickness is revealed as coming directly from Satan. (Job 2:7.) *So Satan went forth and smote Job with sore boils from the sole of his foot to his crown.* Job maintained steadfast faith as he cried out to God for deliverance, and he was healed. (Job 42: 10,12.)

24. Christ declared that the infirm woman was bound by Satan and ought to be loosed. He cast out the *spirit of infirmity,* and she was healed. (Luke. 13:16.)

25. A devil which possessed a man was the cause of his being both blind and dumb. When the devil was cast out, he could both see and talk. (Matt. 12:22.)

26. A demon was the cause of a boy being deaf and dumb and also the cause of his convulsions. When the demon was cast out, the boy was healed. (Mark. 9:17-27.)

27. It is written: *Jesus of Nazareth went about doing good, and healing all that were oppressed of the devil.* (Acts 10:38.)

28. We are told: *The Son of God was manifested, that he might destroy the works of the devil.* (1 John 3:8.) Sickness is part of Satan's works. Christ, in His earthly ministry, always treated sin, diseases, and devils the same. They were all hateful in His sight. He rebuked them all. He was manifested to destroy them all.

29. He does not want the *works of the devil* to continue in our physical bodies. He was manifested to destroy them. He does not want a cancer, a plague, a curse, the *works of the devil*, to exist in His own members. *Know you not that your bodies are the members of Christ.* (1 Cor. 6:15.)

30. Jesus said, *The Son of man is not come to destroy human lives*, but to save them. (Luke 9:56.) Sickness destroys; therefore, it is not from God. Christ came to *save* us (Greek: sozo, meaning to deliver us, to save and preserve us, to heal us, to give us life, to make us whole), but never to *destroy* us.

31. Jesus said, *The thief* (speaking of Satan) *comes not, but to steal, and to kill, and to destroy: I am come that they might have life, and that they might have it more abundantly.* (John 10:10.)

32. Satan is a killer; his diseases are the destroyers of life. His sicknesses are the thieves of happiness, health, money, fame, and effort. Christ came to give us abundant life in our spirits and in our bodies.

33. We are promised the life of Jesus *in our mortal flesh.* (2 Cor. 4:10,11.)

34. We are taught that the Spirit's work is to quicken our *mortal* bodies in this life. (Rom. 8:11.)

35. Satan's work is to *kill*. Christ's work is to *give life*.

36. Satan is bad. God is good. Bad things come from Satan. Good things come from God.

37. Sickness is, therefore, from Satan. Health is, therefore, from God.

38. All authority and power over all devils and diseases was given to every disciple of Christ. (Matt. 10:1; Mark, 16:17.) Since Jesus said, *If you continue in my word, then are you my disciples indeed,* (John 8:31) these Scriptures apply to you today, that is, *if you continue in* (act on) His Word.

39. The right to pray and receive the answer is given to every believer. (John 14:13,14.) *If you shall ask anything in my name, I will do it.* This logically includes asking for healing, if we are sick.

40. *Everyone that asks receives.* (Matt. 7:7-11.) That promise is for you. It includes everyone who is sick.

41. The ministry of healing was given to *the seventy,*who represent the future workers of the church. (Luke 10:1,9,19.)

42. The ministry of healing was given to all *them that believe* the Gospel, or the practicers or doers of the word. (Mark 16:17.)

43. The ministry of healing is committed to *the elders* of the church. (James 5:14.)

44. The ministry of healing is bestowed upon the whole church as one of its ministries and gifts, until Jesus comes. (1 Cor. 12:9,10.)

45. Jesus never commissioned anyone to preach the Gospel without including healing for the sick. He said, *Whatever city you enter, heal the sick that are there.* (Luke 10:8,9.)

46. Jesus said that He would continue His same works through believers while He is with the Father. *Verily, verily, I say to you, the person that believes on me, the works that I do shall he or she do also; and greater works than these shall they do; because I go to my father.* (John 14:12.) This surely includes healing the sick.

47. In connection the Lord's Supper, the cup is taken *in remembrance* of His blood which was shed *for the remission of our sins.* (1 Cor. 11:25.) The bread is eaten *in remembrance* of His body on which were laid our diseases and the stripes by which *we are healed.* (1 Cor. 11:23,24; Isa. 53:5.)

48. Jesus said that certain teachers were *making the word of God of no effect through (their) tradition.* (Mark 7:13.) Human ideas and theories have for centuries hindered the healing part of the Gospel from being proclaimed and acted upon as it was by the early church.

49. One tradition is that God wills some of His children to suffer sickness and that, therefore, many who are prayed for are not healed because it is not His will to heal them. When Jesus healed the demon-possessed boy whom the disciples *could not heal,* (Mark 9:18.) He proved that it is God's will to heal even those who fail to receive healing; furthermore, He assigned the failure to the disciples to cure the boy, not to God's will, but to the disciples' *unbelief.* (Matt. 17:19,20.)

50. The failure of many to be healed today when prayed for is never because it is not God's will to heal them.

51. If sickness is the will of God, then every physician would be a lawbreaker, every trained nurse a defier of the Almighty, and every hospital a house of rebellion instead of a house of mercy.

52. Since Christ came to do the Father's will, the fact that he *healed them all* is proof that it is God's will that all be healed.

53. If it is not God's will for all to be healed, how did *everyone* in the multitudes obtain from Christ what was not God's will for some of them to receive? The Gospel says, *He healed them all.*

54. If it is not God's will for all to be healed, why do the Scriptures state: *With his stripes we are healed and by whose stripes, you were healed.* (Isa. 53:5; 1 Peter 2:24.) How could we and you be declared healed, if it is God's will for some of us to be sick?

55. Christ never refused those who sought his healing. Repeatedly, the Gospels tell us that He healed them all. Christ the healer has never changed.

56. Only one person in the entire Bible ever asked for healing by saying, *If it be your will.* That was the poor leper to whom Jesus immediately responded, *I will; be clean.* (Mark 1:40-41.)

57. Another tradition is that we can glorify God more by being patient in our sickness than by being healed. If sickness glorifies God more than healing, then any attempt to get well by natural or divine means would be an effort to rob God of the glory that we should want Him to receive.

58. If sickness glorifies God, then we should rather be sick than well.

59. If sickness glorifies God, Jesus robbed His Father of all the glory that He possibly could by healing *everyone*, (Luke 4:40.) The Holy Spirit continued doing the same throughout the Acts of the Apostles.

60. Paul says, *You are bought with a price: therefore glorify God in your body, and in your spirit, which are God's.* (1 Cor. 6:20.)

61. Our bodies and our spirits are bought with a price. We are to glorify God in both.

62. We do not glorify God in our spirit by remaining in sin. We do not glorify God in our body by remaining sick.

63. John's Gospel is used to prove that sickness glorifies God. (John 11:4.) But God was not glorified in this case until Lazarus was raised up from the dead, the result of which was, *Many of the Jews believed on him.* (John 11:45.)

64. Another tradition is that while God heals some, it is not His will to heal all. But Jesus, who came to do the Father's will, did *heal them all.*

65. If healing is not for all, why did Jesus bear *our* sicknesses, *our* pains, and *our* diseases? If God wanted some of His children to suffer, then Jesus relieved us from bearing something which God wanted us to bear. But since Jesus came to do the *will of the Father*, and since He *has borne our diseases*, it must be God's will for all to be well.

66. If it is not God's will for all to be healed, then God's promises to heal are not for all. That would mean that faith does not come by hearing the Word of God alone, but by getting a special revelation that God has favored you and wills to heal you.

67. If God's promises to heal are not for all, then we could not know what God's will is by reading His Word alone. That means we would have to pray until He speaks directly to us about each case in particular. We could not consider God's Word as directed to us personally, but would have to close our Bibles and pray for a direct revelation from God to know if it is His will to heal each case.

68. God's Word is His will. God's promises reveal His will. When we read of what He promises to do, we then know what it is His will to do.

69. Since it is written, *Faith comes by hearing the word of God,* then the best way to build faith in your heart that God is willing to heal you is for you to hear that part of God's Word which promises you healing.

70. Faith for spiritual healing *comes by hearing* the Gospel: *He bore our sins.* Faith for physical healing comes *by hearing* the Gospel: *He bore our sicknesses.*

71. We are to *preach the Gospel* (that He bore our sins) *to every creature.* We are to preach the Gospel (that He bore our sicknesses) *to every creature.*

72. Christ emphasized His promise, *If you shall ask anything in my name, I will do it,* by repeating it twice. (John 14:12-14.) He did not exclude healing from this promise. Anything includes healing. This promise is for all.

73. If healing is not for all, Christ should have qualified His promise when He said, *Whatever you desire* (except healing) *when you pray, believe that you receive it, and you shall have it.* (Mark 11:24.) But He did not. Healing, therefore, is included in the whatever. This promise is made to you.

74. If it is not God's will to heal all, His promise would not be dependable where Christ said, *If you live in me, and my words live in you, you shall ask what you will, and it shall be done to you.* (John 15:7.)

75. James says: *Is any sick among you? Call for the elders of the church; and let them pray over them, anointing them with oil in the name of the Lord; and the prayer of faith shall save the sick, and the Lord shall raise them up.* (James 5:14,15.) This promise is for all, including you, if you are sick.

76. If God today has abandoned healing in answer to prayer in favor of healing only by medical science, as modern technology speculates, that would mean that He requires us to use a less successful method during a better dispensation. He healed them all then, but today many diseases are incurable by medical science.

77. Paul tells us that God would have us *prepared to every good work,* (2 Tim. 2:21) *thoroughly furnished to all* good

works, (2 Tim. 3:17) *that we may abound to every good work.* (2 Cor. 9:8.) A sick person cannot measure up to these Scriptures. These conditions would be impossible if healing is not for all. Either healing is for all, or these Scriptures do not apply to all.

78. Bodily healing in the New Testament was called a mercy, and it was God's mercy which always moved Him to heal all the sick. His promise is that He *is plenteous in mercy to all that call on Him.* (Ps. 86:5.) That includes you, today.

79. The correct translation of Isaiah 53:4 is: *Surely* (or certainly) *He has borne our sicknesses, and carried our pains.* To prove that our sicknesses were carried away by Christ, just like our sins were carried away, the same Hebrew verb for *borne* and *carried* is used to describe both. (Isa. 53:4, 11,12.)

80. Christ *was made to be sin for us* (2 Cor. 5:21) when He *bore our sins.* (1 Peter 2:24.) He was *made a curse for us* (Gal. 3:13) *when he bore our sicknesses.* (Matt. 8:17.)

81. Since Christ *bore our sins,* how many is it God's will to forgive? Answer: *Whoever believes.* Since Christ *bore our sicknesses,* how many is it God's will to heal? Answer: *He healed them all.*

82. Another tradition is that if we are righteous, we should expect sicknesses as a part of our life. They quote the Scripture: *Many are the afflictions of the righteous,* (Ps. 34:19) but this does not mean sicknesses as some would have us believe. It means trials, hardships, persecutions and temptations, but never sicknesses or physical disabilities.

83. It would be a contradiction to say, "Christ has borne our sicknesses, and with His stripes we are healed," but then add, "Many are the sicknesses of the righteous, which He requires us to be bear."

84. To prove this tradition, theologians quote, *But the God of all grace, who has called us to his eternal glory by Christ Jesus, after that you have suffered for a while, make you perfect, establish strengthen and settle you.* (1 Peter 5:10.) This suffering does not refer to suffering sickness, but to the many ways in which God's people have so often had to suffer for their testimony. (Acts 5:41; 2 Cor. 12.)

85. Another tradition is that we are not to expect healing for certain afflictions. People quote the Scripture, *Is any among you afflicted? let him or her pray.* (James 5:13.) This again does not refer to sickness, but to the same things pointed out in number 82.

86. Another tradition is that God chastises His children with sickness. The Scripture is quoted, a part of which says, *Whom the Lord loves he chastens.* (Heb. 12:6-8.) God does chasten those whom He loves, but it does not say that He makes them sick. The word *chasten* here means "to instruct, train, discipline, teach, or educate," like a teacher "instructs" a pupil, or like a parent "trains" and teaches a child.

87. When a teacher instructs a student, various means of discipline may be employed, but never sickness. When a parent trains a child, there are many ways to chasten, but never by imposing a physical disease upon it. For our Heavenly Father to *chasten* us does not require that He lay a disease upon us. Our diseases were laid upon Christ. God could not require that we bear, as punishment what Jesus has substantially borne for us. Christ's sacrifice freed us forever from the curse of sin and disease which He bore on our behalf.

88. The most common tradition is the worn-out statement: The age of miracles is past. For this to be true, there would have to be a total absence of miracles. Even one miracle would prove that the age of miracles is not past.

89. If the age of miracles is past, no one could be born again because the new birth is the greatest miracle a person can experience.

90. If the age of miracles is past, as some claim, that would mean that all the technical evidence produced in hundreds of laboratories of the world, concerning innumerable cases of miraculous healings, is false and that God's promises to do such things are not for today.

91. Anyone who claims that the age of miracles is past denies the need, the privileges, and the benefits of prayer. For God to hear and answer prayer, whether the petition is for a postage stamp or for the healing of a paralytic, is a miracle. If prayer brings an answer, that answer is a miracle. If there are no miracles, there is no reason for faith. If there are no miracles, prayer is mockery and only ignorance would cause anyone to either pray or expect an answer. God cannot answer prayer without a miracle. If we pray at all, we should expect that prayer to be answered. If that prayer is answered, God has done it; and if God has answered prayer, He has performed something supernatural. That is a miracle. To deny miracles today is to make a mockery of prayer today.

92. The age of miracles is not past because Jesus, the miracle-worker, has never changed: Jesus Christ *the same yesterday and today and forever.* (Heb. 13:8.)

93. When Jesus sent His disciples to preach the Gospel, He told them: *These* (supernatural) *signs shall follow them that believe.* This was for *every creature,* for *all nations,* until *the end of the world.* The end of the world has not yet come, so the age of miracles has not passed. Christ's commission has never been withdrawn or canceled.

94. Christ's promise for the spirit — that it shall be saved — is in His commission and is for all. His promise for the body — that it shall recover — is in His commission and

is for all. To deny that one part of His commission is for today is to deny that the other part is for today. As long as Jesus' commission is in effect, the unsaved can be healed spiritually and sick people can be healed physically by believing the Gospel. Multiplied thousands of sincere people all over the world are receiving the benefits of both physical and spiritual healing through their simple faith in God's promises.

95. Christ bore your sins so that you may be forgiven. Eternal life is yours. Claim this blessing and confess it by faith; God will make it good in your life.

96. Christ bore your diseases so that you may be healed. Divine health is yours. Claim this blessing and confess it by faith; God will manifest it in your body.

97. Like all of Christ's redemptive gifts, healing must be received by simple faith alone without natural means and, upon being received, must be consecrated for Christ's service and glory alone.

98. God is willing to heal believers as He is to forgive UNbelievers. (Rom. 8:32.) That is to say, if when you were unsaved, God was willing to forgive you, now that you are His child, He is willing to heal you. If He was merciful enough to forgive you when you were UNconverted, He is merciful enough to heal you now that you are in His family.

99. You must accept God's promise as true and believe that you are forgiven before you can experience the joy of spiritual healing. You must accept God's promise as true and believe that you are healed before you can experience the joy of physical healing.

100. *As many* (sinners) *as received him were born of God.* (John 1:12,13.) *As many* (sick) *as touched him were made whole.* (Mark 6:56.)

When we preach that it is always God's will to heal, the question is immediately raised: "How then could we ever die?"

God's word says: *You take away their breath, they die, and return to their dust.* (Ps. 104:29.) The Bible says: *You shall come to your grave in a full age, like as a shock of corn comes in its season.* (Job 5:26.)

For us to come to our full age and for God to take away our breath does not require the aid of a disease. God's will for your death as His child is that, after living a fruitful life, fulfilling the number of your days, you simply stop breathing and fall asleep in Christ, to awaken on the other side and live with Him forever. *So shall* (you) *ever be with the Lord.* (1 Thess. 4:17) Indeed, this is the blessed hope of the righteous.

> **Because you have set your love upon me, God says, therefore will I deliver you: I will set you on high, because you have known my name. You shall call upon me, and I will answer you: I will be with you in trouble; I will deliver you, and honor you. With long life will I satisfy you, and show you my salvation.**
>
> **Ps. 91:14-16**

6
31-Day Healing Devotional

Day 1

Words of Health and Healing

Pleasant words are as an honeycomb, sweet to the soul, and health to the bones.

Proverbs 16:24

The time to learn the power of faith-filled words is when you are experiencing good health and feeling great. Don't wait until you are sick to start speaking words of health and vitality over your body.

Jesus said in Mark 11:23, *"He shall have whatsoever he saith."* Therefore start saying today, "Based on the Word of God, Jesus bore my sicknesses and carried my diseases. For this reason, every organ, muscle and fiber of my body functions and operates properly, as God intended it. My youth is renewed like the eagles. He redeems my life from destruction and I have strength and energy to accomplish that which my Heavenly Father has called me to do." Each day speak words of faith and power over your body. They will be health to your bones!

CONFESSION: My tongue speaks health, healing and energy to my body. It speaks words of life and not sickness. I speak health, therefore, I walk in health and strength.

Day 2

Look to the Word of God for Healing

**But Naaman was wroth, and went away, and said,
Behold, I thought, he will surely come out to me and
stand and call on the name of the Lord his God and
strike his hand over the place and recover the leper.**

2 Kings 5:11

Sometimes in seeking an answer from God, especially
in the area of healing, we so often try to figure out how God
is going to meet our need. We want to know, "How is He
going to answer my prayer?" "How is my body going to
feel after my brothers and sisters have laid hands on me?"
"What is going to happen when I am anointed with oil?" In
the above Scripture we read that Naaman was angry with
Elisha because he did not come out and make an spectacular
scene to bring about his healing. Finally, at the encour-
agement of his servants, Naaman simply obeyed the
instructions of the man of God. The result was that his flesh
came again like unto the flesh of a little child and he was
clean.

The basis for faith concerning healing is not how you
feel when hands are laid on you, or whether you go to the
altar to receive prayer. Rather, your anchor needs to be the
instructions from the Word of God. Don't miss the
supernatural by looking for the spectacular.

CONFESSION: My faith is based and anchored on the
Word of God. I will follow God's instructions and be
blessed with the results that He has promised.

Day 3

It Is God's Will To Heal

...He that hath seen me hath seen the Father. . . .
                                                    John 14:9

Always remember that it is God's will to heal the sick. Some Christians believe and say, "Maybe the Lord put this sickness on me for some reason or purpose." Ask yourself, "Did Jesus ever put sickness on anyone while He was on the earth?" "Did Jesus ever refuse or turn anyone away?" "Did we ever hear Jesus say, 'Now, you keep this sickness a little longer so that you will learn a lesson?' " Not one time! If you want to know God's will, you must look and listen to Jesus. He went about doing good and healing. (Acts 10:38.) We can pray in faith and assurance knowing that healing is the Father's will for us — His children.

CONFESSION: I know, based upon the Word of God, that healing is God's will for me. I rest assured that as I pray according to the Word and will of God, He hears me. Because He hears me, I know that I have the petition that I desire of Him.

Day 4
Seven Things To Remember About Healing

1. Settle This Fact — It is God's Will To Heal You

The same Bible that says He forgives all our iniquities also says that He heals all our diseases. (Psalm 103:3.)

2. Sickness and Disease Do Not Come From God

Jesus went about doing good and healing all. God does not need sickness and disease to teach you a lesson — that is why He gave us His Word.

3. See Yourself Well

See yourself as having that which the Word says is yours. Saturate your spirit and mind with the Word of God concerning healing and the healing will begin from the inside out!

4. Establish a Release Point for Your Faith

A release point may be the day hands are laid on you — or after you have been anointed with oil. Establish a point of reference, "From now on I believe I have received my healing."

5. Remember Faith Is Now

God is ready today. He wants you to receive your healing today. Don't wait around thinking, "Maybe someday I'll get healed." Reach out by faith and take what is yours.

6. Don't Talk Defeat

From the moment you release your faith for healing, don't talk defeat, sickness or disease again. Don't talk about how you *feel*; talk about what you *believe*.

7. Stay in the Word

The devil may come with thoughts of doubt and unbelief. Resist him by staying in the Word. Fill your mind and spirit each day with Scriptures concerning healing.

CONFESSION: It is God's will to heal me. He uses His Word. I refuse to speak sickness and disease. Daily, I strengthen myself with God's Word.

Day 5

God's Medicine

The words that I speak unto you, they are spirit, and they are life.

John 6:63

In the last twenty years, medical science has developed some amazing breakthroughs in the area of medicine and different types of surgery. Many sicknesses, which were once life threatening, are now curable or at least held at bay by drugs or medical procedures. But there is still a more effective type of medicine: the Word of God. Proverbs 4:22 says, *"God's Words are life, health and healing to all your flesh."* When your doctor prescribes medicine, you read the instructions, follow directions and take it regularly. You must also take God's medicine with the same dedication — read the instructions, follow directions and regularly put God's Word in your spirit. The Word of God regarding healing that has been placed within your spirit will keep God's healing power working in you.

CONFESSION: God's Words are life, health and healing to all my flesh. As I put God's medicine into my spirit regularly, it keeps my body well, strong and able to be victorious over sickness and disease.

Day 6

He Will Keep His Word

God is not a man, that he should lie: neither the son of man, that he should repent: hath he said, and shall he not do it? Or hath he spoken, and shall he not make it good?

Numbers 23:19

No word that has ever come from God can return to Him void. (Isaiah 55:11.) You can rest assured that whatever Scripture you are standing on for your healing contains enough power to bring about the manifestation you need. God said in Jeremiah 1:12,"...*I will hasten my Word to perform it.*" God watches over His Word to perform it and make it good. As you act and stand upon God's Word concerning healing, or anything else you might need, you can be sure God is watching over His Word to perform it in your life.

CONFESSION: God watches over His Word to perform it in my life. His Word does not return unto Him void, but accomplishes that which pleases Him. I stand upon His promises and He makes them good in my life.

Day 7

By His Stripes You Were Healed

Who His own self bare our sins in His own body on the tree, that we, being dead to sins, should live unto righteousness, by whose stripes ye were healed.

1 Peter 2:24

When the enemy brings to you thoughts of doubt such as, "You're not going to get your healing this time," just say aloud, "I don't have to get my healing — Jesus already got it for me because 1 Peter 2:24 says, *'..by His stripes I was healed.'* " Isn't it wonderful to realize that the healing of your body was purchased for you 2000 years ago by the stripes of Jesus at Calvary? We do not have to beg, plead or talk God into healing us. All we have to do is reach out by faith and take what was bought and paid for at a precious price by our Lord and Saviour, Jesus Christ.

CONFESSION: The Bible says that I was healed by the stripes of Jesus. Therefore, I receive what Jesus bought for me. I am healed. His promise is mine now.

Day 8

Getting in Position To Receive

Confess your faults one to another, and pray for one another, that ye may be healed.

James 5:16a

This Scripture says that we should not only confess our faults one to another, but that we are to pray one for another that we might be healed. God is telling us that by praying for someone else, you can be healed! This is the principle of sowing and reaping. If you need healing, start praying for those around you who need healing. If you have unconfessed sin in your life, by all means go to the Lord as commanded by 1 John 1:9. Confess your sin and get it out of your life. If you have wronged a brother or have ought against anyone, go to them and talk with them about it so that you can be freed. Only then will you have confidence and boldness to pray for the healing of others. A clean heart puts you in a position to receive healing for yourself.

CONFESSION: As I pray for healing for others, healing comes back to me. I confess and release all sin that is present in my life right now. I release any resentment, bitterness or anything I might have against anyone right now. Healing is mine. I will not allow sin to stand in the way of my healing manifestation.

Day 9

Be Strong in Faith

And being not weak in faith he considered not his own body now dead, when he was about an hundred years old neither yet the deadness of Sarah's womb: he staggered not at the promise of God through unbelief, but was strong in faith giving Glory to God.

Romans 4:19,20

Abraham faced natural facts that could have prevented him from believing God. Today, we too face natural circumstances. Abraham knew there was no natural way for God's promise to him to come to pass. Yet the Bible says that Abraham considered not his own body. He ignored the natural, physical evidence around him and believed only God's Word. He made a decision to commit to the Word of God regardless of what he saw. Today you and I need to take the same approach Abraham did. Start with the Word of God, search out the promises of God and believe what He has said about your need. Meditate on those promises until they sink down into your spirit. From then on talk only as if your healing or miracle had already happened. And finally, give praise and glory to God for your miracle. He will come through for you.

CONFESSION: I purpose to walk according to the promises of God. I will not stagger at His Word through unbelief. Instead, I am strong in faith, giving glory to God, being fully persuaded that His Word will come through for me.

Day 10

Jesus Is Still the Healer

How God anointed Jesus of Nazareth with the Holy Ghost and with power: Who went about doing good, and healing all that were oppressed of the devil; for God was with him.

Acts 10:38

Who does this verse say anointed Jesus? God did! What did Jesus do with the anointing that He received from God the Father? He went about doing good and healing. We can see in this verse that it was actually God Who healed the people when Jesus healed, because it was God Who had anointed Jesus. Jesus said, "*...the Father that dwelleth in me, he doeth the works*" (John 14:10). God is a healing God! He does not afflict with sickness and disease. Who did Jesus heal? The Bible says that He healed all *that were oppressed.* All includes everybody. All would have included you and me if we had lived in that day and if we would have been sick. The good news is that Jesus is still in the healing business.

CONFESSION: Healing is good. Jesus is still in the healing business. Jesus is my Saviour and my Healer.

Day 11

Don't Look at the Wind

But when he saw the wind boisterous, he was afraid; and beginning to sink, he cried, saying, Lord, save me. And immediately Jesus stretched forth His hand and caught him and said unto him, O thou of little faith. Wherefore didst thou doubt?

Matthew 14:30,31

The Bible says that we are not to be ignorant of Satan's devices. One of the enemy's main tactics is to tempt you to take your eyes off the Word of God. He will try everything he knows to get you to concentrate on your physical senses instead of focusing on the promises of God. When Peter took his eyes off the word *"come"* and started looking at the storm, he started to sink. He started to focus on what his physical senses were telling him instead of on what Jesus said. Don't let the same thing happen to you. Once you appropriate a promise from the Word of God on healing, hang on to it. Focus on that promise and nothing else. Remember that the enemy will try to steal that word or promise from you. Be ready to resist him and to hang on to it. Don't let go. The Word of God will bring the harvest.

CONFESSION: I will keep my eyes upon the Word of God. I am not moved by what I see, hear or feel. I am moved only by what I believe and I believe the Word of God.

Day 12

Let Freedom Ring

And as ye go, preach, saying, the Kingdom of Heaven is at hand. Heal the sick, cleanse the lepers, raise the dead, cast out devils: freely ye have received, freely give.

Matthew 10:7,8

There are some people who want you to believe that diseases such as AIDS are God's ways of judging or punishing the human race today. But as we find in Scripture, God is the healer not the afflictor. (Acts 10:38.) The enemy has promoted this lie. If people believe God is the cause of their disease, they will be driven away from God's mercy and compassion. This is where you and I come in. We need to tell people with any disease that Jesus is Lord and wants to be their Healer. We need to tell them that God loves them and has the desire and power to make them well. The good news that we must get out to the masses — through television, radio and the printed page — is that God is not their captor, He wants them to be free.

CONFESSION: My God, my Heavenly Father, is a good God. He is a loving God with compassion for those who are sick and hurt. I will do my part in spreading the good news that our God is a God of love, power and mercy. I believe that God will make Himself real and alive in their life.

Day 13

The Lord's Commission for the Lost and for the Sick

And He said unto them, go ye into all the world and preach the gospel to every creature...and these signs shall follow them that believe; in my name...they shall lay hands on the sick and they shall recover.

Mark 16:15,17,18

Can you tell by looking at this passage of Scripture how to select those who you are to lay hands on? Will Jesus appear in a vision and say, "There is one of the lucky ones. Lay hands on him but not on her. She needs to stay sick awhile longer." No. It just says lay hands on the sick. So if it is the will of God for some to remain sick, then obeying this Scripture would be in opposition to the will of God. If that is the case, the Scripture would have had to say something like, "They shall lay hands only on those people who God wants healed, and they shall recover." But it doesn't say that. Jesus said exactly what He meant. We have been assigned to *preach the Gospel to every creature and lay hands on the sick* — period!

CONFESSION: Jesus tells me to preach the Gospel and to lay hands on the sick. When I lay hands on the sick in Jesus' name, they shall recover. Jesus works with me confirming His Word with signs following. I provide the hands; God provides the healing.

Day 14

Jesus Paid the Price

That it might be fulfilled which was spoken by Esaias the prophet, saying, himself took our infirmities and bare our sicknesses.

Matthew 8:17

Jesus took our infirmities and bore our sicknesses. I am included in the word *"our."* He took *my* infirmities and bore *my* sicknesses! You have to apply the Word of God and make it personal in your life. Agree with the Word of God daily and say, "Regardless of what I see or feel, I am healed and my body has to align itself with the Word of God because Jesus took my infirmities and bore my sicknesses." Since Jesus Himself took our infirmities and bore our sicknesses, we don't have to bear any disease. He took them so that we could be free.

CONFESSION: Jesus bore my sicknessess, so there is no need for me to have them. I make a quality decision to walk in this freedom and accept what Jesus has provided for me.

110

Day 15

A Prescription for Healing

Is any sick among you? Let him call for the elders of the church; and let them pray over him, anointing him with oil in the name of the Lord: and the prayer of faith shall save the sick; and the Lord shall raise him up and if he have committed sins, they shall be forgiven him.
James 5:14,15

In this passage of Scripture James asks if there are any sick among the people in the church. Is the word *any* all inclusive? Yes, it is — it includes you and me. The above verse gives specific instructions on how to receive healing. We can conclude that it *must* be God's will to heal any who are sick in the Church. This is one of God's prescriptions for receiving healing. Notice that the Word says that the prayer of faith *shall* save the sick. It doesn't say that the prayer of faith *might* save the sick. It doesn't say the prayer of faith *can* save the sick. It says the prayer of faith *shall save the sick and the Lord shall raise him up*. Who does the raising up? Who does the healing? The Lord, no one else. Always remember this truth.

CONFESSION: It is God's will to heal any sick that are in the Church — His body. I am a member of the Body of Christ and it is God's will for me to be well and to walk in good health.

Day 16

Your Covenant With God

Thou shalt therefore keep the commandments, and the statutes, and the judgments, which I command thee this day, to do them. Wherefore it shall come to pass, if ye hearken to these judgments and keep and do them, that the Lord thy God shall keep unto thee the covenant and the mercy which he sware unto thy fathers: And he will love thee, and bless thee, and multiply thee: he will also bless the fruit of thy womb, and the fruit of thy land, thy corn, and thy wine, and thine oil, the increase of thy kine, and the flocks of thy sheep, in the land which he sware unto thy fathers to give thee. Thou shalt be blessed above all people: there shall not be male or female barren among you, or among your cattle. And the Lord will take away from thee all sickness, and will put none of the evil diseases of Egypt, which thou knowest, upon thee; but will lay them upon all *them* that hate thee.

Deuteronomy 7:11-15

What does this Scripture passage have to do with us today? God is the same God today as He was back then. The Scripture says that He does not change. God was against sickness and disease in the Old Testament and God is against sickness and disease in the New Testament. God made provision for healing for the children of Israel. As long as they served the Lord and walked according to His commandments and statutes, He took sickness away from the midst of them. Matthew 8:17 says that Jesus *bore our sicknesses and took our pains*. The same God who made provision for His people —the children of Israel — many years ago under the Old Covenant, has also made provision for our healing under the New Covenant.

CONFESSION: Jesus, my Lord, bore my sicknesses and carried my pains. I have a covenant of healing with God my Heavenly Father. There shall no evil befall me and no plague come near my dwelling and the number of my days will be fulfilled.

Day 17

Don't Be Misled (Part 1)

The following Scriptures are used by teachers who are opposed to the idea that it is God's will to heal. They often misinterpret these verses to prove that there are times when God wants you to be sick.

1. Many are the afflictions of the righteous: But the Lord delivers them out of them all (Psalms 34:19). This verse does not say many are the sicknesses and diseases of the righteous. The word "affliction," as used in this verse, has nothing to do with sickness or disease. It means persecutions, hardships and trials. Christ did not bear our persecutions, trials and hardships. However, He did bear our sins and sicknesses. (Matt. 8:17.)

2. Whom the Lord loves He chasteneth and scourgeth every son whom He receiveth. If ye endure chastening, God dealeth with you as with sons; for what son is he whom the Father chasteneth not? But if ye be without chastisement whereof all are partakers, then are ye bastards and not sons (Heb. 12:6-8). This Scripture does not say, "Whom the Lord loves He makes sick or strikes with the plague." The word "chasten" comes from a Greek word meaning "to instruct, train, discipline, or teach," similar to a teacher instructing a student or a parent teaching their child. When parents train their children, they may use various methods to guide them in the way they should go. But a loving mother or father would never use a sickness or disease.

This subject is continued on the next day.

Day 18
Don't Be Misled (Part 2)

3. But the God of all grace, who has called us to His eternal glory by Christ Jesus, after that you have suffered a while make you perfect, stablish, strengthen, settle you (1 Peter 5:10).

This Scripture does not say that after you have been sick and suffered with a disease long enough, God will make you mature and establish you in the faith. Keep in mind there were many ways Paul suffered, as recorded in the Book of Second Corinthians, which didn't include sickness or disease. Paul mentioned persecutions, imprisonments, tumults, reproaches and a number of others. Paul endured these sufferings for the sake of winning others to Christ. But suffering with sickness is not mentioned.

4. Lest I should be exalted above measure through the abundance of the revelations, there was given to me a thorn in the flesh, the messenger of Satan to buffet me, lest I should be exalted above measure (2 Cor. 12:7).

This particular Scripture passage has been used for many years to prove that sometimes you have to endure sickness and disease. Here are just a few statements to think about concerning this topic:

• The term "thorn *in the flesh*" is used in the Old Testament as an illustration of a personality and not a sickness. (Num. 33:55; Josh. 23:13.)

• Paul's thorn was a messenger of Satan — a being, not a sickness.

• When Paul mentions his many sufferings for Christ in 2 Corinthians 11, he does not mention sickness and disease.

For additional teaching on Paul's thorn, read *Messenger of Satan* by Charles Capps, Harrison House Publishers, Tulsa, Oklahoma.

CONFESSION: I serve a God Who desires His children to walk in truth. I walk in the light of the Word and will not be deceived by those who would knowingly or unknowingly misinterpret the Scriptures.

Day 19

Whatsoever Includes Healing

And in that day ye shall ask me nothing. Verily, verily I say unto you, whatsoever ye shall ask the Father in my name, He will give it you. Hitherto have ye asked nothing in my name. Ask and ye shall receive, that your joy may be full.

John 16:23,24

In this Scripture Jesus gives us direction on how to have our prayers answered. He didn't say to ask Him for "it." He didn't say to pray for "Jesus' sake." He didn't say to beg your Heavenly Father for what you need. He said *whatsoever* — including healing — *ye shall ask the Father in my name, He will give it you.* Jesus didn't say He *might* give it you or He *can* give it to you. He said He *will give it you.* He said, *"Ask and ye shall receive."* You can have full assurance that when you ask the Father in Jesus' name for His healing power to operate in your body, He will give it to you. Jesus goes on to say, . . .*that your joy may be full.* God wants you full of joy today — not full of sickness and disease. So, *ask and ye shall receive!*

CONFESSION: Whatsoever I ask my Heavenly Father in Jesus' name, He gives it to me. When I pray and ask my Father for His healing power in Jesus' name, I receive and my joy is made full in Him.

Day 20

Believe That You Will Receive

There I say unto you, what things soever ye desire, when ye pray, believe that ye receive them, and ye shall have them.

Mark 11:24

And this is the confidence that we have in Him, that if we ask anything according to his will, he heareth us; and if we know that he hear us, whatsoever we ask we know that we have the petitions that we desired of him.

1 John 5:14,15

Here are two more Scripture passages that you can stand on to receive your healing. In the first Scripture Jesus said, *"What things soever ye desire."* That would include healing, wouldn't it? When did Jesus say you should believe? After your symptoms leave? After the fever breaks? After the doctor gives you a good report? No! You believe you receive your healing when you pray!

First John 5:14,15 tells us that we have this confidence or assurance in God, that if we ask anything according to His will (which includes healing), He hears us. Since we know he hears us, whatsoever we ask (again, including healing), we know that we have those requests or petitions from Him. Prayer is a God-given means through which we can receive healing. Therefore, ask and believe you receive when you pray and it is yours.

CONFESSION: What things soever I desire, when I pray, I believe that I receive them, and I shall have them. I have this assurance in my Father, that when I ask anything according to His will, which is His Word, He hears me. Since He hears me, I am confident that I have the request I desire from God.

Day 21

Don't Forget the Benefits

Bless the Lord, O my soul, and forget not all His benefits; who forgiveth all thine iniquities; who healeth all they diseases; who redeemeth thy life from destruction; who crowneth thee with loving kindness and tender mercies; who satisfieth thy mouth with good things; so that thy youth is renewed like the eagle's.

Psalm 103:2-5

When we go to work for a company, one of the first things we want to know about is the benefits they offer. Along with the salary, we want to know about vacation time, health insurance and any other area that might benefit us or our families. Yet, so many Christians ignore or fail to check into God's benefits. *"Who forgiveth all thine iniquities"* is a benefit that Christians have embraced and appropriated. However, they have forgotten or have not claimed the benefit of *"who healeth all thy diseases."* The good news is that God wants to forgive us of our sins and make us a new creation in Christ. He also wants to heal our physical body. Get into God's Word today and search for the blessings that your Heavenly Father has provided for you. Don't forget your benefits.

CONFESSION: I make a decision this day to walk in the blessings and benefits my God has provided for me. He has forgiven all my iniquities. He has healed all my diseases. He redeems my life from destruction. He crowns me with loving kindness and tender mercies. He satisfies my mouth with good things so that my youth is renewed like the eagle's.

Day 22

No Fear, No Evil, No Plague

He that dwelleth in the secret place of the most high shall abide under the shadow of the Almighty. I will say of the Lord, *He* is my refuse and my fortress; my God in Him will I trust. Thou shalt not be afraid for the terror by night, *nor* for the arrow that flieth by day, *nor* for the pestilence that walketh in darkness, *nor* for the destruction that wasteth at noonday. A thousand shall fall at thy side, and ten thousand at thy right hand, but it shall not come nigh thee. There shall no evil befall thee, neither shall any plague come nigh thy dwelling. For He shall give His angels charge over thee, to keep thee in all thy ways. They shall bear thee up in their hands, lest thou dash thy foot against a stone. With long life will I satisfy him and shew him my salvation.

Psalms 91:1,2,5-7,10-12,16

You should read Psalm 91 and confess it over your life and your family daily. Though fear may be all around, verses 5 and 6 remind you that you don't have to be afraid, because God is your refuge and your fortress. Verses 7 through 10 assure you that no evil or, as some translations put it, *"no calamity or accident shall befall you for He has given His angels charge over you."* Every morning, before you or your family start the day, confess that the angels are standing in charge over them and that they are safe and protected by the authority of the Word of God. And, finally, stand against any plague or sickness that would try to come against you. That disease, according to verse 10, has no right to even come near you. As warriors of Jesus Christ we need to confess Psalm 91 aloud and put up a hedge of protection around ourselves and our loved ones daily. Be satisfied with long life and see the salvation of God!

CONFESSION: Go to your Bible and look up Psalms 91. Personalize it and confess it over yourself and your family.

Day 23

You Are the Redeemed

Christ hath redeemed us from the curse of the law,
being made a curse for us.

Galatians 3:13

If you read Deuteronomy 28, you will find a number of sicknesses and diseases mentioned as a result of people walking in disobedience to God's statutes and laws. Just in case any sickness or disease wasn't mentioned from verse 16 through verse 60, verse 61 says, "*Also every sickness and every plague which is not written in the book of this law.*" All diseases are definitely included, period. But, thank God Galatians 3:13 says, "*Christ hath* (hath means He has already done it) *redeemed us from the curse of the law, being made a curse for us.*" Whose sin did Jesus take on the cross? It wasn't any of His — it was yours and mine. Then whose sicknesses and diseases did He take? Yours and mine! He did it to redeem us from the curse of the law so that the blessings of Abraham might come on the gentiles through Jesus Christ. I don't know about you, but I want all the blessings of Abraham I can get my hands on. Psalms 107:2 says, "*Let the redeemed of the Lord say so....*" Declare your redemption today!

CONFESSION: I am the redeemed of the Lord and I am saying so. Christ has redeemed me from the curse of the law, being made a curse for me. I am redeemed form every sickness and every disease and the blessings of Abraham are overtaking me from this day forward.

Day 24

Roadblocks to Healing (Part 1)

The following might be some reasons why people may fail to receive their healing. It is our prayer that this checklist be of value to anyone who may be struggling in these areas.

1. Not being rooted and grounded in the Word of God concerning healing.

The Bible says that faith comes by hearing and hearing by the Word of God. (Romans 10:17.) Quite possibly there have been some who have sought healing without a firm Scriptural foundation. Jesus said that some would hear the Word of God and receive it with joy (possibly on healing) but when tribulation or persecution (maybe symptoms) arise because of the Word they are offended (or give up). (Matt. 13:20,21)

2. Not following the instructions as they are given in the Word of God.

The basis for anyone's faith for healing or anything else from God is the Word of God — not what you think it says, not what your best friend or relative says is in the Bible, but what the Bible actually says. We must follow the instructions down to the letter. The Bible says to be doers of the Word. (James 1:22.)

For example, Jesus said, *"Whatsoever ye shall ask the Father in my name, He will give it you"* (John 16:23) Many are still praying for Jesus' sake. In James 5:14, there are specific instructions that are to be followed for healing. The person who is sick must call the elders. The elders are to pray and anoint with oil in the name of the Lord. The Lord will raise him up.

This subject is continued on the next Day.

Day 25

Roadblocks to Healing (Part 2)

3. Don't ignore or break God's natural laws.

Another reason why some have failed to receive healing is due to ignoring or breaking God's natural laws of health and nutrition. It is presumptuous and foolish to think we can ask God for healing while we eat foods that harm our body. The same is also true for lack of rest, proper sleep and exercise.

4. Iniquity in your heart.

You cannot expect God's blessings in your life if, knowingly, you operate in unconfessed sin or hold bitterness and resentment in your heart toward another person.

5. Not properly discerning the Lord's body.

In 1 Corinthians 11:27-31, the Bible tells us to examine ourselves as we take communion — to judge ourselves so that we won't be judged. Verses 29 and 30 tell us because of not properly discerning the Lord's body, many are weak and sick. As we take communion, let us first examine our hearts and also consider the price that was paid for our spiritual and physical redemption.

CONFESSION: I make a decision this day to make God's Word the final authority in my life. I will not harbor resentment or unforgiveness in my heart toward anyone. I refuse sin in my life. I determine to eat right, get plenty of sleep and exercise. I will resist getting caught up in stress, worry and fear in my life. I examine and judge myself so I won't be judged and I will properly discern the Lord's body and His sacrifice for me.

Day 26

Agree on Healing

Again I say unto you, that if two of you shall agree on earth as touching anything that they shall ask, it shall be done for them of my Father which is in heaven. For where two or three are gathered together in my name, there am I in the midst of them.

Matthew 18:19,20

In this Scripture passage we can see the power that prayer has when two or more believers agree concerning a particular need. You can receive physical healing for your body by acting upon this Scripture. Just do what Jesus said to do. All you need is one other believer who will agree with you, so that when you pray to receive God's healing power, you will receive it. Jesus said, *"as touching anything that they shall ask."* That would include physical healing, wouldn't it? Jesus went on to say, *"it shall be done for them of my Father which is in heaven."* It says that it *shall be done*, not that it *might be done*. Jesus also promised He would be in the midst, or in the presence, of two or more believers who are joined together in faith in His name. There is power in unity and this promise is available to meet your need today!

CONFESSION: When I agree in prayer with a fellow believer according to Matthew 18:19 concerning anything we ask, it shall be done for us by our Father which is in heaven. Jesus is in our midst as we act upon His Word.

Day 27

Having a Healthy Spirit, Soul and Body

And the very God of peace sanctify you wholly; and I pray God your whole spirit and soul and body be preserved blameless unto the coming of our Lord Jesus Christ.

1 Thessalonians 5:23

Webster's Dictionary defines wholeness as, "not broken or injured; intact; unimpaired-entire; complete." Wholeness is God's will for each and every person. God wants your spirit to be sound and well. This is accomplished by continuing to feed upon the Word of God. The Lord also wants your soul to be healthy and well. Your soul is made up of your mind, your will and your emotions. Negative influences that affect the soul are worry, fear, resentment, unforgiveness, to name just a few. It is God's will for you to be mentally and emotionally sound. 2 Timothy 1:7 says, *"For God hath not given us the spirit of fear; but of power and of love and of a sound mind."* God has provided health and healing for your body through Christ Jesus. Whatever you may be facing, the Lord desires you to be made whole and complete in Him.

CONFESSION: My God has made provision for me to be well in spirit, soul and body. His Word, living and abiding in me, makes my spirit strong. Jesus is Lord over my mind, will and emotions. Therefore, my soul is well. Jesus bore my sickness and carried my diseases and I am complete and made whole in Him.

Day 28

Our Father's Care

If ye then, being evil, know how to give good gifts unto your children, how much more shall your Father which is in heaven give good things to them that ask Him?

Matthew 7:11

Every good gift and every perfect gift is from above, and cometh down from the Father of lights with whom is no variableness, neither shadow of turning.

James 1:17

Set some time aside today and think about what a loving and caring God we serve. You and I have a Heavenly Father so anxious to bless us and provide all the things we need. Romans 8:32 says, *"He that spared not His own Son, but delivered Him up for us all, how shall He not with Him also freely give us all things? "* Our Father has many good gifts, one of which includes healing for our bodies. Acts 10:38 says, *"Jesus went about doing good and healing all that were oppressed."* If you are standing on the Word of God for your healing, nothing will help your faith more than to continually think about your Heavenly Father's love and care for you. Therefore, today, rest in your Father's care and concern for you.

CONFESSION: My Heavenly Father has provided good gifts for me. He has blessed me with all spiritual blessings in Christ Jesus. My Heavenly Father has a deep care and concern for me. I will walk in His peace.

Day 29

There Is Healing In His Name

...Silver and gold have I none; but such as I have give I thee. In the name of Jesus Christ of Nazareth rise up and walk. And he took him by the right hand and lifted him up and immediately his feet and ankle bones received strength. And his name through faith in his name hath made this man strong....

Acts 3:6,7,16

There is power in the name of Jesus. There is healing in the name of Jesus. Notice that Peter did not pray for the man, he did not anoint him with oil. Peter just used the name of Jesus and commanded the man to rise and walk. Philippians 2:9,10, say, *"God hath highly exalted Him and given Him a name which is above every name: that at the name of Jesus every knee should bow..."* The name of Jesus is above the names of cancer, arthritis, diabetes, and every other sickness and disease. Jesus said, *"all power is given unto me in heaven and in earth, go ye therefore"* (Matthew 28:18,19.) He has commissioned us to go to the world, equipped with His name, to set the captives free.

CONFESSION: As a believer, I have been given the authority to use the name of Jesus. As I exercise this authority on earth, all of Heaven backs me up. At the name of Jesus every sickness and every disease must bow and give up their strongholds.

Day 30

Gifts of Healing

For to one is given by the Spirit the word of wisdom; to another the word of knowledge by the same Spirit; to another faith by the same Spirit, to another gifts of healing by the same Spirit.

1 Corinthians 12:8-9

Many are healed and set free by the power of God through the gifts of healing. They operate as the Spirit wills, not by the will of man. (1 Corinthians 12:11.) There are a number of ways for people to be healed, but the gifts of healing work differently from the other methods. It is still God's healing power, but in most instances the recipient is not standing on the Word for their healing; they haven't been anointed with oil; it just comes to them automatically. As you look through the Gospels, you will see Jesus operating in the gifts of healing many times. Please keep in mind, this method of healing is as the Spirit wills, not by anything you do. God is so gracious to provide more than one way for you and I to receive our healing.

Note: For additional study of the gifts of healing and the rest of the gifts of the Spirit, read *The Holy Spirit and His Gifts* by Kenneth Hagin, Kenneth Hagin Ministries, Tulsa, OK.

CONFESSION: My God desires all to be healed and to walk in divine health. God has placed the gifts of healing in the church and, as a result, many are healed. Even if I do not receive my healing by this means, my Father God has graciously supplied other ways for me to be healed.

Day 31

Stand Your Ground

Wherefore take unto you the whole armor of God, that ye may be able to withstand in the evil day, and having done all, to stand: stand therefore. . . .
Ephesians 6:13,14a

. . .be not slothful, but followers of them who through faith and patience inherit the promises.
Hebrews 6:12

As we walk by faith in this world, there will be challenging times. It is inevitable. Things may get a little tough at times but rest assured you will come out on top if you refuse to faint or give up. There will come a point in your faith walk, when you have to stand and act as though what God says is true even when you can't feel it or see it working on your behalf. As you fight the good fight of faith, allow patience to have her perfect work so that you hold steady and inherit the promises of God. Satan will continually try and convince you that your situation is hopeless. He will bring thoughts of doubt and fear. It's up to you to cast down imaginations and all things contrary to God's Word. So when you are tempted to quit and cave in, remember God has promised that He will always cause you to triumph in Christ Jesus!

CONFESSION: I refuse to quit. I refuse to cave in. I will not be slothful, but I will be a follower with them who through faith and patience inherit the promises. I will cast down all thoughts that do not agree with God's Word. My God always causes me to triumph in Christ Jesus.

*J*esus has given you the right to use His name. That name can break the power of disease, the power of the adversary. That name can stop disease and failure from reigning over you. There is no disease that has ever come to man which this name cannot destroy.⁴

E. W. Kenyon

7

Prayers for Healing

Prayer for Personal Healing Concerns

Father, in the name of Jesus, I confess Your Word concerning healing. As I do this, I believe and say that Your Word will not return to You void, but will accomplish what it says it will. Therefore, I believe in the name of Jesus that I am healed, according to 1 Peter 2:24, **Who his own self bare our sins in his own body on the tree, that we, being dead to sins, should live unto righteousness; by whose stripes we were healed.** It is written in Your Word, in Matthew 8:17, that Jesus Himself took our infirmities and bore our sicknesses. Therefore, with great boldness and confidence I say on the authority of that written Word that I am redeemed from the curse of sickness, and I refuse to tolerate its symptoms.

Satan, I speak to you in the name of Jesus and say that your principalities, powers, your spirits who rule the present darkness, and your spiritual wickedness in heavenly places are bound from operating against me in any way. I am the property of Almighty God, and I give you no place in me. I dwell in the secret place of the Most High God. I abide, remain stable and fixed under the shadow of the Almighty, whose power no foe can withstand.

I confess the Word of God abides in me and delivers to me perfect soundness of mind and wholeness in body and spirit from the deepest parts of my nature in my immortal spirit even to the joints and marrow of my bones. That Word is medication and life to my flesh for the law of the

Spirit of life operates in me and makes me free from the law of sin and death.

I have on the whole armor of God, and the shield of faith protects me from all the fiery darts of the wicked. Jesus is the High Priest of my confession, and I hold fast to my confession of faith in Your Word. I stand immovable and fixed in full assurance that I have health and healing now in the name of Jesus.

Once this has been prayed, thank the Father that Satan is bound and continue to confess this healing and thank God for it.

Prayer for Another Person in Need of Healing

Father, in Jesus' name, I pray and ask for a manifestation of Your healing power to flow into _____'s body right now. Father, Your Word tells us in James 5:16 to pray one for another that we may be healed. I believe, based upon Your Word, that it is your will that _____ be made whole physically, spiritually, mentally and in every area of _____'s life.

Father, as your Word reads in Ephesians 1:18, I ask that _____'s eyes be open to the full understanding and knowledge that healing is his/hers today. I pray that _____ will have a complete revelation of Your healing power and the redemptive work of Jesus upon the cross for our healing.

I thank You now, Father, for healing _____in Jesus' name.

Healing Concordance

Genesis

    20:17 and God healed Abimelech

Exodus

    15:26 I am the Lord that healeth thee

    23:25 I will take sickness away from the midst of thee

Leviticus

    13:18 even in the skin thereof, was a boil, and is healed

    13:37 the scall is healed, he is clean

    14:48 because the plague is healed

Numbers

    1:8-9 every one that is bitten, when he looketh upon it, shall live

    23:19 shall he not make it good?

Deuteronomy

    5:33 that ye may prolong your days

    7:15 take away from thee all sickness

    30:19 therefore choose life, that both thou and thy seed may live

    30:20 for he is thy life, and the length of thy days

    32:39 and I heal

2 Kings

    5:14 and his flesh came again like unto the flesh

1 Chronicles

    28:28 and he died in a good old age

2 Chronicles

7:14 and will heal their land

16:12 yet in his disease he sought not to the Lord

30:20 and healed the people

Job

5:26 thou shalt come to thy grave in a full age

37:23 he will not afflict.

42:10 gave Job twice as much as he had before

Psalms

30:2 O and thou hast healed me

34:19 the Lord delivereth him out of them all

41:3 strengthen him upon the bed of languishing

41:4 heal my soul

86:5 for thou, Lord, art good, and ready to forgive

91:1 shall abide under the shadow of the Almighty

91:2 He is my refuge and my fortress

91:6 nor for the pestilence

91:10 neither shall any plague come

91:15 I will be with him in trouble

91:16 with long life

103:3 who healeth all thy diseases

105:37 there was not one feeble person

107:20 He sent his word, and healed them

147:3 He healeth the broken in heart

Proverbs

3:2 for length of days, and long life

4:22 for they are life...and health to all their flesh

9:11 the years of thy life shall be increased

12:18 but the tongue of the wise is health

14:30 the life of the flesh

16:24 and health to the bones

17:22 a merry heart doeth good like a medicine

Isaiah

19:22 and shall heal them.

40:29 He giveth power to the faint

40:31 the LORD shall renew their strength...they shall walk, and not faint

41:10 I will strengthen thee

53:5 with his stripes we are healed

55:11 it shall not return unto me void

58:8 thine health shall spring forth speedily

Jeremiah

3:22 I will heal your backslidings

17:14 and I shall be healed

30:17 I will restore health unto thee

33:6 I will bring it health and cure

Lamentations

2:13 who can heal thee?

Ezekiel

47:9 they shall be healed

Hosea

> **6:1** and he will heal us

Malachi

> **3:6** I am the LORD, I change not

> **4:2** arise with healing in his wings

Matthew

> **4:23** and healing all manner of sickness

> **4:24** and he healed them.

> **7:7** ask, and it shall be given you

> **8:3** and immediately his leprosy was cleansed

> **8:17** Himself took our infirmities, and bare our sicknesses

> **9:2,7** thy sins be forgiven thee...and he arose

> **9:35** healing every sickness and every disease among the people

> **10:1** to heal all manner of sickness

> **10:8** heal the sick, cleanse the lepers, raise the dead

> **11:5** the blind receive their sight, and the lame walk, the lepers are cleansed, and the deaf hear, the dead are raised up

> **12:13** and it was restored whole

> **12:15** and he healed them all

> **12:22** and he healed him, insomuch that the blind and dumb both spake and saw

> **14:14** and he healed their sick

> **14:36** and as many as touched were made perfectly whole

15:30 and he healed them

17:20 and nothing shall be impossible unto you

18:20 there am I in the midst of them

19:1 and he healed them there

20:34 immediately their eyes received sight

21:14 and he healed them.

Mark

1:31 and immediately the fever left her

1:34 he healed many that were sick of divers diseases

1:42 the leprosy departed from him, and he was cleansed

2:12 immediately he arose, took up the bed

3:5 and his hand was restored whole as the other

3:15 power to heal sicknesses, and to cast out devils

5:34 and be whole of that plague

5:41 I say unto thee, arise

6:56 as many as touched him were made whole

9:27 Jesus took him by the hand, and lifted him up; and he arose

10:52 thy faith hath made thee whole

10:52 immediately he received his sight

11:24 what things soever ye desire, when ye pray, believe that ye receive them, and ye shall have them.

16:18 they shall lay hands on the sick, and they shall recover

Luke

4:18 to heal the brokenhearted

4:18 recovering of sight to the blind

4:18 to set at liberty them that are bruised

4:39 and immediately she arose

4:40 he laid his hands on every one of them, and healed them

5:13 and immediately the leprosy departed

6:10 stretch forth thy hand...his hand was restored whole

6:18 vexed with unclean spirits...were healed

6:19 there went virtue out of him, and healed them all

7:10 found the servant whole that had been sick

9:1 power and authority over all devils, and to cure diseases

9:2 to heal the sick

9:6 and healing every where

9:11 healed them that had need of healing

10:9 and heal the sick that are therein

10:19 nothing shall by any means hurt you

13:12 woman, thou art loosed from thine infirmity

13:13 and immediately she was made straight

14:4 and he took him, and healed him, and let him go

17:19 arise, go thy way: thy faith hath made thee whole

18:42 receive thy sight: thy faith hath saved thee

18:43 immediately he received his sight

John

4:50 go thy way; thy son liveth

5:6 Wilt thou be made whole?

5:8 rise, take up thy bed, and walk

5:9 immediately the man was made whole

9:6 he anointed the eyes of the blind man with the clay

9:7 he went his way therefore, and washed, and came seeing

14:13 whatsoever ye shall ask in my name, that will I do

15:7 it shall be done unto you

16:24 ask, and ye shall receive, that your joy may be full

Acts

3:6 in the name of Jesus Christ of Nazareth rise up and walk

3:7 and immediately his feet and ankle bones received strength

5:16 and they were healed every one.

8:7 many taken with palsies, and that were lame, were healed

9:34 arise, and make thy bed...and he arose immediately

10:38 healing all that were oppressed of the devil

14:10 stand upright on thy feet. And he leaped and walked

19:12 the diseases departed from them

27:34 for this is for your health

Romans

4:20 he staggered not at the promise of God through unbelief

4:21 what he had promised, he was able also to perform.

8:32 shall he not with him also freely give us all things?

10:17 faith cometh by hearing

1 Corinthians

12:28 then gifts of healings, helps, governments, diversities of tongues

Galatians

3:13 Christ hath redeemed us from the curse of the law

1 Thessalonians

5:23 preserved blameless unto the coming of our Lord Jesus Christ

Hebrews

13:8 Jesus Christ the same yesterday

James

1:17 every good gift and every perfect gift is from above

5:14 is any sick among you?

5:15 and the prayer of faith shall save the sick

5:16 pray one for another, that ye may be healed

1 Peter

2:24 Who his own self bare our sins in his own body... by whose stripes ye were healed

1 John

5:14 if we ask any thing according to his will, he heareth us

3 John

1:2 prosper and be in health, even as thy soul prospereth

Recommended Reading

Available From Harrison House

Christ the Healer, F.F. Bosworth.

God's Creative Power for Healing, Charles Capps.

God's Will For Healing, Gloria Copeland.

You Are Healed, Kenneth Copeland.

Healing Belongs to Us, Kenneth Hagin.

How To Live and Not Die, Norvel Hayes.

Be Healed, Marilyn Hickey.

Jesus the Healer, E.W. Kenyon.

Healing the Sick, T.L. Osborn.

Healed of Cancer, Dodie Osteen.

How To Minister Healing To The Sick, John Osteen.

Available From Other Sources

Divine Healing, Andrew Murray, Whitaker House, Springdale, PA

The Balm of Giliad, Lilian B. Yeomans, Radiant Books, Gospel Publishing House, Springfield, MO

The Great Physician, Lilian B. Yeomans, Radiant Books, Gospel Publishing House, Springfield, MO

Healing From Heaven, Lilian B. Yeomans, Radiant Books, Gospel Publishing House, Springfield, MO

Health and Healing, Lilian B. Yeomans, Radiant Books, Gospel Publishing House, Springfield, MO

Study Notes

Study Notes

Study Notes

Study Notes

Healing Register

"Surely he hath borne our griefs, and carried our sorrows: yet we did esteem him stricken, smitten of God, and afflicted.

"But he was wounded for our transgressions, he was bruised for our iniquities: the chastisement of our peace was upon him; and with his stripes we are healed."

Isaiah 53:4,5

Healed of	Date

Healing Register

"Surely he hath borne our griefs, and carried our sorrows: yet we did esteem him stricken, smitten of God, and afflicted.

"But he was wounded for our transgressions, he was bruised for our iniquities: the chastisement of our peace was upon him; and with his stripes we are healed."

Isaiah 53:4,5

Healed of   **Date**

_____   _____

_____   _____

_____   _____

_____   _____

_____   _____

_____   _____

_____   _____

_____   _____

_____   _____

_____   _____

_____   _____

_____   _____

_____   _____

_____   _____

_____   _____

_____   _____

_____   _____

Healing Register

"Surely he hath borne our griefs, and carried our sorrows: yet we did esteem him stricken, smitten of God, and afflicted.

"But he was wounded for our transgressions, he was bruised for our iniquities: the chastisement of our peace was upon him; and with his stripes we are healed."

Isaiah 53:4,5

Healed of   Date

_____ _____

_____ _____

_____ _____

_____ _____

_____ _____

_____ _____

_____ _____

_____ _____

_____ _____

_____ _____

_____ _____

_____ _____

_____ _____

_____ _____

_____ _____

References

The Amplified Bible (AMP). Old Testament section copyright © 1965, 1987 by Zondervan Corporation. New Testament section copyright © 1958, 1987 by The Lockman Foundation. Used by permission.

The Bible. A New Translation (Moffatt). Copyright © 1950, 1952, 1953, 1954 by James A.R. Moffatt. Harper & Row Publishers, Inc., New York, New York.

The Holy Bible: New International Version (NIV). Copyright © 1973, 1978, 1984 by International Bible Society. Used by permission of Zondervan Publishing House. All rights reserved.

New American Standard Bible (NAS). Copyright © by The Lockman Foundation 1960, 1962, 1963, 1968, 1971, 1972, 1973, 1975, 1977. Used by permission.

The New King James Version of the Bible (NKJV). Copyright © 1979, 1980, 1982 by Thomas Nelson, Inc., Publishers. Used by permission.

Strong's Exhaustive Concordance of the Bible by James Strong, copyright © 1987 by Baker Book House, Grand Rapids, Michigan.

Weymouth's New Testament in Modern Speech (Weymouth), by Richard Francis Weymouth, Harper & Row Publishers, Inc., New York, New York.

The Holy Bible (Knox) translated by Monsignor Ronald Knox. Copyright © 1944, 1948, 1950 by Sheed & Ward, Inc., New York.

The Twentieth Century New Testament. Copyright © 1901 by Fleming H. Revell Company, New York and Chicago. All rights reserved.

The New Testament: A Private Translation in the Language of the People by Charles B. Williams (Williams). Copyright © 1937 by Bruce Humphries, Inc. Copyright assigned, 1949 to The Moody Bible Institute of Chicago.

Endnotes

[1]*Healing From Heaven*, Radiant Books-Gospel Publishing House, Springfield, Missouri

[2]*Divine Healing*, Whitaker House, Springdale, PA

[3]*The John G. Lake Sermons on Dominion Over Demons, Disease and Death*, Edited by Gordon Lindsay, Published by Christ for the Nations, Dallas, TX

[4]*Jesus the Healer*, Kenyon Gospel Publishing Society, Lynnwood, WA.

Additional copies of
God's Word for Your Healing

are available from your local bookstore
or from:

Harrison House
P. O. Box 35035
Tulsa, Oklahoma 74135

For additional copies
of this book
in Canada contact:

Word Alive
P. O. Box 670
Niverville, Manitoba
CANADA R0A 1EO

The Harrison House Vision

Proclaiming the truth and the power
Of the Gospel of Jesus Christ
With excellence;

Challenging Christians to
Live victoriously,
Grow spiritually,
Know God intimately.